D1008164

HOW TO
SELF-PUBLISH
a Book on
AMAZON.COM

Chris McMullen

How to Self-Publish a Book on Amazon.com:

Writing, Editing, Designing, Publishing, and Marketing

Revised, Updated, and Expanded in March, 2014

Cover Design by Melissa Stevens
www.theillustratedauthor.net
Write. Create. Illustrate.

CreateSpace

Third Edition (March, 2014)
Second Edition (May, 2013)
First Edition (May, 2009)

ISBN: 1442183012
EAN-13: 9781442183018

Nonfiction > Reference > Publishing
Nonfiction > Reference > Authorship

Contents

THIS BOOK WAS first published in 2009. Much has changed between then and now. For example, CreateSpace and BookSurge have merged together; now there is just one company, CreateSpace, which combines the services of both. Microsoft Word 2010 is available, where many of the features are quite different from the 2003 edition. More and more books are being self-published as eBooks in addition to paperbacks, whereas this book was originally geared primarily toward paperback self-publishing – and the formatting of eBooks is considerably different from the formatting of paperbacks. Also, the world of marketing has changed considerably over the past few ways – especially, ways to achieve this effectively without being a salesperson or spending money on advertising — and the author has experienced these changes firsthand.

Hence the need for this edition: **to significantly update the content**.

This book should answer the vast majority of your publishing questions, but in case it doesn't answer *all* of them, try asking your questions on the CreateSpace community forum. There are many knowledgeable self-publishers (including the author of this book) and small publishers who frequently share their expertise there.

Introduction

I HAVE SELF-PUBLISHED over a dozen books on Amazon.com using CreateSpace, a print-on-demand self-publishing service and member of the Amazon group of companies. I have considered reasons for self-publishing versus searching for a publisher or literary agent. I have edited and formatted several manuscripts to turn them into published books. I have designed most of my own covers, but also have experience working with a cover designer. I have learned tips for making books more marketable, and explored a variety of marketing strategies.

But it wasn't all easy: I have run across numerous issues, especially formatting my books into PDF files and having the final product match my vision. Having solved several formatting and editing problems and delivered numerous books to market myself, it occurred to me that it might be useful for other aspiring authors to have a self-publishing guide available to them.

My publishing experience started when I was half-way through writing a book on extra dimensions – a subject I really enjoy contemplating. I read various books on how to get published. I wrote a query letter and invested many hours in writing a lengthy book proposal – which was very much like a book itself. And then I embarked on the daunting task of convincing an editor or literary agent to publish my work.

After I had begun my search in 2008, a new link on Amazon's website caught my interest: in regards to self-publishing a book on Amazon.com. I clicked the link and learned about CreateSpace, a print-on-demand publishing service that is a member of the Amazon group of companies. I read this information over a few times and considered the prospects of self-publishing versus working with a publisher.

There were several advantages of self-publishing a book that would be available on-demand which appealed to me immediately:

- I wouldn't need to invest any money.
- My book would be on the market in a month, not a year or longer.
- I could publish my work the way I like it; I wouldn't need to revise it until I found an angle that appealed to an editor, nor would an editor ask me to change it.
- I would save myself from the hassles of finding a literary agent or editor willing to work with me.

Prior to this, when I had considered self-publishing, I had ruled it out because I thought it would require a large investment and much entrepreneurship. However, CreateSpace's self-publishing service would save me from a financial investment and the problem of how to get my book to market: If someone buys my book on Amazon, CreateSpace prints the book and ships it out. One beautiful aspect of print-on-demand is that you don't need to have a garage full of books to self-publish.

I still had some concerns about self-publishing. If I could get published, I expected the publisher to print thousands of books and pay a royalty up-front based on this. Through self-publishing, I would instead get paid as the books sell and there would be no guarantee that a certain number would sell. So I saw both pros and cons.

Obviously, I finally decided to self-publish my books. Two more ideas weighed in on this. First, I noticed that if I self-published my book on Amazon, it would be available for several years to come; whereas the book may soon go out of print with a regular publisher. I wanted to share my work for many years, not just a couple of years. Next, I had a backlist of material that I had been writing for 20 years: I decided to edit and self-publish some of these books to better acquaint myself with the publishing process and test the print-on-demand concept out. It worked out well for me and I have since self-published several books; I have also collaborated on professional projects with other authors and designers.

Self-publishing on Amazon.com may or may not be the best option for you. Several ideas in the first chapter can help you decide this for yourself. The remaining chapters aim to help you with your entire project, from developing the concept for your book to editing your manuscript to making your work available on the market to promoting your book.

I hope that you find this book helpful. I wish you success in your writing and publishing endeavors.

Sincerely,

Chris McMullen

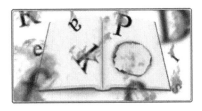

Disclaimer

THE INFORMATION IN this book is presented as accurately as possible based on policies and practices that were put in place at the time of publication (most recently, in 2014). The policies and practices of various companies, such as self-publishing companies, are subject to change. The author makes no guarantees regarding the information contained in this book. However, the author has worked hard to ensure that the information is as accurate as possible as of the time of publication. You should check directly with the companies themselves in order to receive the most up-to-date, accurate information about their policies, practices, pricing, etc.

CreateSpace and Amazon are trademarks of Amazon.com, Inc. These and other trademarks and brands referred to in this book are property of their respective owners; these companies did not endorse this book and the opinions expressed in this book are not necessarily shared by these companies.

1 Reasons for Self-Publishing

CHOOSING WHETHER TO self-publish, search for a literary agent, or directly contact a publisher that doesn't require an agent is an important decision for an author to make – one that an aspiring author does not wish to regret later. Let us consider the advantages and disadvantages of print-on-demand self-publishing versus searching for a publisher that will distribute your book to the market.

Print-on-Demand

This new concept is becoming increasingly popular, especially on Amazon.com. Instead of printing a large number of your books and storing them in a warehouse, a print-on-demand self-publishing company prints and binds your book as soon as it sells online. In this way, you are able to avoid the large investment that would otherwise be required to publish a book yourself.

Advantages of Self-Publishing on Amazon

(1) No investment is required if you publish a book with CreateSpace, a print-on-demand self-publishing company and member of the Amazon group of companies.

You'll probably spend more money (and time and effort) on books that teach you how to write a book proposal and list addresses of publishers (unless you borrow these from a library) and the postage to cover the dozens of query letters, self-addressed stamped envelopes, book proposals, and manuscripts that you will need to send to various publishing houses and/or literary agents.

(2) Your book can be on the market in as little as a week.

Once your book is written, you need only make it into two PDF files – one for the book interior and one for the cover – as described in Chapter 7. A couple of days after you submit your PDF files, you can order a proof of your book (for as little as about two dollars plus shipping). Your proof will arrive in about a week. If you are happy with your proof, you go online to approve your proof, and then you will be able to find it in searches on Amazon.com in a few days, where it will be available for sale around the world.

If instead you publish with a publisher that prints thousands of copies of your book and distributes physical copies to bookstores across the nation, it often takes six months to a year before your book hits the market.

This is especially important if you are publishing a nonfiction book with time-sensitive information. For example, if you are writing a book about how to survive in the real estate market in a tough economy, you want your book on the market before the economy rebounds.

(3) Save yourself from the hassles of contacting publishers and agents, and from the prospect of numerous rejection letters.

When you self-publish, you don't have to sell your work to a publisher or agent. You don't have to perfect the art of writing an effective, eye-catching query letter.

You don't have to learn how to write a book proposal that identifies your target audience and convinces an editor that your book will sell very well. And you don't have to deal with rejection letters.

Instead, you can focus on writing your book. You can put the emphasis of being an author on the writing itself, not on being a salesman. (However, applying some marketing techniques, as described in Chapter 10, will help you increase sales; but this is something you are expected to do whether or not you self-publish.)

(4) Self-publish with a company you trust: Amazon.

You don't have to self-publish your book by investing a large amount of money in a publishing company you've never heard of. Now you can self-publish with a company that is part of the Amazon group of companies, and without the investment.

(5) Publish your book just the way you like it.

You don't need to modify the concept of your book in order to appeal to an editor's preferences. To you, your book is a work of art. It's your baby. Through self-publishing, you don't have to sacrifice features of your book in order to reduce the cost of printing your book or make your book more marketable in the editor's eyes. You can be your own boss.

On the other hand, your book may sell better if an editor suggests or requires you to modify your book. Even if you self-publish, you should first test-market your book to receive valuable feedback from others (Chapter 8). You should consider the suggestions that they make – and prepare yourself to handle constructive criticism well – as they represent a sample of how others will view your work.

(6) You can leave your book on the market indefinitely.

When you publish a book with CreateSpace, it remains available indefinitely (though you may choose to make it unavailable at any given time). So readers may purchase new copies of your book at Amazon.com for many years to come.

Most publishing companies print a limited number of copies and only print new copies or new editions for a limited period of time – only for as long as the publisher feels that there is sufficient demand. Many books go out of print after about a year, since demand is often greatest shortly after the book is released onto the market. However, those rare books that are popular over a long period may remain on the market for several years.

(7) Revisions are easy to make, and you can make them immediately.

If you spot a typo, printing error, or other mistake after you make your book available, you can make it immediately unavailable until the problem is corrected. To correct the problem, you submit a revised PDF file in the same way that you submitted the original, order a new proof, and once you are happy with the proof, you approve it and the book becomes available once again. Of course, you should examine your first proof carefully to avoid the need for corrections, but if you find the need to make revisions, it is quick and easy to do.

You can also update your book as needed without creating a new edition. However, if you do this, you should consider the possible ramifications of different readers discussing your book and realizing that their copies are not quite the same. You might include a printing number (e.g. third printing) on the copyright page to help distinguish slightly different copies.

A publisher that prints numerous copies of your book and then distributes them will expect your first proof to be final. You are stuck with what you get unless your book is successful enough to warrant new editions.

(8) It's okay if you change your mind after making your book available.

You're not committed to self-publishing once you begin it. Even after receiving an ISBN and making your book available on Amazon.com, if you publish with CreateSpace you can retire your book – just choose to make it no longer available for sale at Amazon.com. You are free to change your mind and try the traditional publishing route. This affords you some flexibility, in case you have reservations about print-on-demand self-publishing. You can try it out with virtually zero investment. (Amazon may choose to leave your book's photo and description available on their website, and may allow readers who have a copy of your book to sell their used books on their webpage.)

(9) You can choose to promote your book as little or as much as you like.

There is no pressure to promote your book. If you write a book proposal, editors generally expect to see a description of promotional strategies that you will engage in that will help to market your book. The publishers are already investing a large sum of money to print and distribute copies of their books, and so are not willing to make additional large investments to promote all of their books. They are more likely to do this for authors who have proven success or celebrity status. Publishers expect other authors to invest time and money in their own books, including self-promotion. This can include radio or television appearances, presentations with back-of-the-room sales, writing promotional articles or soliciting book reviews, using part of your advance to purchase copies and sell them directly, maintaining a website, and so on.

If you want to focus more on the writing and spend less time with the business side of authorship – i.e. feel less like a salesman – then self-publishing can help you relieve this sense of external pressure to promote your book. However, any promotional activities you are willing to perform will help you increase sales (Chapter 10). But you don't have to make promises for how much promotion you will undertake, there are ways to help promote your book with zero or minimal investment, and there is no rush to promote your book heavily when it first comes on the market (although marketing can sometimes be more effective when a book is released). Because print-on-demand self-publishing with Create-Space allows you to keep your book on the market indefinitely, you can start out with little or no promotion and gradually promote your book more and more, if you wish. This way, you can see firsthand to what degree, if any, your promotional activities are affecting sales. If you see it helping significantly, you are apt to be more motivated to promote your book.

(10) You can still distribute physical copies to bookstores if you want.

While you can make your print-on-demand self-publishing book available on Amazon.com, you can still buy and distribute copies to bookstores. Authors can purchase copies directly from the publisher at a cheap price: At CreateSpace, books with a black-and-white interior start at about two dollars for up to one hundred pages, and then cost about a penny a page after that, while color interior books run about three-fifty for up to forty pages and about seven cents a page beyond that. You can order as little or as much as you want (there is no discount for ordering large quantities – or look at it this way: there is no extra charge for ordering small quantities), and distribute them to bookstores.

Print-on-demand self-published books have virtually no chance of being stocked nationally in chain bookstores. However, there are favorable prospects of local bookstores stocking a few copies of your book. The best way to achieve this isn't through CreateSpace's Expanded Distribution channel (that helps to expand your online presence through online booksellers), but by approaching local bookstores in person with copies of your book on-hand and a press release kit. If your book appears professional and marketable, that's a big plus. You can also approach libraries and other stores that specialize in other products, but also sell books (sometimes those stores are more receptive).

(11) If you have your own webpage, you can include a link to your CreateSpace eStore or your book's product page at Amazon.com.

If you have a webpage for your book, or are willing to get and maintain one, you can include a link to your book at Amazon.com and if you publish with Create-Space, you can include a link directly to your book's CreateSpace eStore. You earn a higher royalty when customers buy your book at CreateSpace (which will only be found if you provide a link to it), but they may be more willing to buy your book at Amazon.com since this name is much more recognizable. You can start a free website/blog at WordPress.com, for example (and turn it into a professional-looking domain name for an additional fee).

(12) You can skip the struggle of breaking through the publishing industry as a first-time author.

The publishing industry is very competitive. Millions of people are willing to write a book that will appear in bookstores (physical or online) and sell. Publishers are swarmed with more query letters and book proposals than they can read. The largest publishers do not accept unsolicited manuscripts, book proposals, or even query letters; you need a good agent just to get your foot in. It is difficult, and can be time-consuming, to get a publisher interested in your work, and similarly challenging to find a good agent to represent you. It is especially hard to break through as a first-time author. Many publishers and agents are not willing to take a chance on a first-time author, and so do not consider their requests at all. They have enough query letters and book proposals to consider already, so they can afford to be quite selective.

But you can put your first book on the market through print-on-demand self-publishing. If your book becomes moderately successful, you may be able to use the success of your first book to get a publisher interested in a second book; they might even be willing to publish your first book if you sell enough copies over a six-month period (it can be a selling point). Though if your book is successful, you might feel even more compelled to self-publish subsequent books.

Disadvantages of Self-Publishing on Amazon

(1) You won't receive an advance on your royalties.

When you elect to publish your book with a print-on-demand self-publisher, you receive your royalties as you sell your books. (Actually, you typically get paid for a month's royalties at the end of the following month.) You don't receive any money until after a book sells.

Publishers sometimes offer authors advances on their royalties. The amount of the advance depends upon the author and the book; the publisher is not apt to risk losing money by paying too large of an advance. If you are a celebrity or if you are already a successful author, you have good prospects for receiving a rather large advance.

But if you had celebrity status or have already published several books, chances are that you wouldn't be reading this book. For the rest of us, it's a challenge just to get published, and then the advance may not be too large. Part of the advance would probably be invested toward promoting the book, and part may cover probable book expenses anticipated by the publisher – e.g. travel expenses to take photographs for the book.

However, a traditional publisher would likely pay you some amount upon receipt of your completed manuscript based on probable sales from the number of books they intend to initially print and distribute. Unless they have reason to print a large number of copies, though – i.e. some reason to expect your book to be very successful – this might not translate to a large advance.

If you're not anticipating a large advance, the lack of an advance on your royalties may not be too important.

(2) Being self-published isn't quite the same as being published.

Having a publisher accept your manuscript for publication, offer you a contract, distribute physical copies of your book to bookstores, and pay you royalties in the traditional manner carries some status – a respectable accomplishment in the eyes of some.

Self-publishing your work bypasses the editorial review process. You can publish anything, whether or not it is good or useful. Having an editor accept your book for publication signifies that your work is worthy of being published.

But it would be naïve to assume that a book is not good simply because it was self-published. On the contrary, when a book is sold through Amazon.com, all buyers have the opportunity to post reviews of the book. So if a book does not meet readers' expectations, it will receive poor reviews. This customer review process is one means of establishing the quality of a book. A reviewer can also submit a book review to a newspaper, magazine, or website.

In this way, many books are self-published and highly regarded. The worth of the book is measured by what's actually between the covers, which can be measured regardless of whether or not it went through the editorial publishing process.

In fact, some traditionally published books turn out to be flops; so having a publisher accept a manuscript for publication does not necessarily provide a measure of the book's quality.

Still, there is some perceived status with the traditional publication process. It's more important if this status means something to *you* than if it is important to other people you know.

(3) If your first book is published through the traditional route and becomes successful, it will be easier to publish subsequent books and you will probably command higher advances on the royalties.

Looking ahead to future books, if you have high expectations for a very successful first book – considering many other books that will be written by already popular authors in this competitive market – then if you are able to publish your first book with a traditional publisher, you may have better opportunities available when you are ready to publish subsequent books. Of course, this means that first you must have your first book accepted for publication and that it also needs to be as successful as you envision.

If you have a highly successful first book that is self-published, you may still be able to advertise this as a selling point when trying to get a second book published. If you self-publish and build a good name for yourself, the audience that you have already created may be looking for subsequent works; so self-publishing subsequent works may still be a good option.

(4) There might be some book features that you could get from a publisher that you can't get by self-publishing on Amazon.com.

Self-publishing on Amazon.com presently offers a full-color or black-and-white interior with a full-color cover. CreateSpace only offers softcover for publishing on Amazon (although hardcover is an option with a significant up-front fee and expense, but hardcover books published through CreateSpace won't be available on Amazon unless you fulfill orders yourself through Amazon Advantage, for example). You can choose between white and off-white pages, and glossy or matte covers. There are a variety of sizes to choose from, from as small as 5" x 8" to as large as 8.5" x 11".

However, if you want a smaller or larger book, a trim size that's not available, a hardcover book, a spiral bound book, embossed lettering on the cover, any other feature that is not offered, then you either have to sacrifice the feature or find an alternative publisher. Some traditional publishers may offer more options.

(5) Print-on-demand self-publishing might not be the best option for producing super low-priced books.

You can purchase books directly for a pretty good price (starting at about two dollars for a hundred black-and-white pages or about three-fifty for forty color pages), and you receive pretty good royalties (sixty percent minus the cost of the book). However, there is a minimum price that you can charge for your book (which is higher for color than for black-and-white, and which depends on your page count). You can still make a book reasonably cheap if you want – say, around five dollars for a black-and-white interior that is not too long. But if you want to make a very inexpensive book – say, under four dollars – this will be difficult to do. Or if you want to publish in color and keep the cost down, if you have a large number of pages, this may also turn out not to be manageable. Going with a publisher that is willing to print and distribute a large number of books (e.g. mass market) may help you keep the price down. So if you're writing a book for which there is already a lot of low-priced competition, print-on-demand self-publishing may not be the best option.

For most books, though, print-on-demand self-publishing is a relatively inexpensive process, and you can set a very fair price and still keep a larger than normal royalty. If you sell fewer copies than you would through traditional publishing, a larger royalty helps to compensate for part of this difference. We'll consider how to set the prices in Chapter 9. The point here is how print-on-demand self-publishing might not be the best option for producing very low-priced books (but most books do not fall into this category).

A better way to compete in the low-price market may be with eBooks. You can publish an eBook with Kindle, for example, in addition to a paperback with

CreateSpace. In fact, this is something you should consider regardless of your price-point, in order to maximize your book's exposure (unless you're writing a workbook or other book where eBooks aren't practical).

(6) If you are writing a nonfiction book or textbook for which you have expertise and a strong resume or image, you may be able to draw on your expertise in order to get published more easily and draw a higher advance on your royalties.

Some nonfiction and textbook publishers are looking for authors with expertise, experience, and strong qualifications to publish books. If you fall into this category, you can also advertise your expertise in your book description and back cover as a self-published author, but you might find better opportunities in traditional publishing and have an easier time getting published. However, even this field is growing competitive, so if your degree is new, you are inexperienced, or your resume and image are not yet strong, you might still find it challenging to get your work published regardless of your expertise.

(7) You need to create PDF files for your cover and interior in order to use CreateSpace.

If you publish with a traditional publisher, you just have to focus on writing the book. Many publishers will accept a physical manuscript printed on paper; some may prefer a file, but often with some freedom in the format of the manuscript.

However, CreateSpace only accepts PDF files. It is pretty easy to convert a document to PDF (as described in Chapter 7), and it is quite manageable to make a cover and convert it to PDF, too. Even if you have trouble with this, chances are that you can find someone knowledgeable enough with computers to help you out (though you should find what you need to know in Chapter 7). For technical reasons, PDF files do not always print exactly as they look on the screen, as sometimes happens with certain color images (yet this problem is also addressed in Chapter 7).

So you shouldn't be worried about making PDF files – but if you are, you can find free helpful information on CreateSpace's community forum. There are also many free PDF converters available online.

You can focus on writing your book (versus formatting), and completely avoid the issue of making PDF files, by getting published – but then you still won't be concentrating solely on writing your book because you then have to divert some of your energy to query letters and book proposals.

Suppose you do publish your book, or maybe you have already published a book, and it goes out of print. At this point you may be able to self-publish your book on Amazon.com. You should check on the legal details yourself, though. If you are publishing a book now, you might inquire about the prospects for self-publishing the same book once it goes out of print.

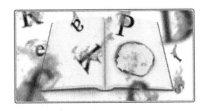

2 Developing the Concept

BEFORE YOU WRITE a book, you should decide whether you want to write fiction or nonfiction. For fiction, you should decide whether you want to write prose or poetry. For prose, you can choose from romance, science fiction, fantasy, horror, etc. Similarly, with nonfiction, you can choose from subjects such as science, how-to, games, computers, photography, cooking, and so on. But whatever your format and subject, you should consider the concept before you write. Even if you have already written your book, you may want to consider the concept, and potential revisions, before you publish your work.

There is an exception: An author who envisions himself or herself as an artist may write in the spirit of Edgar Allen Poe, and create a written work of beauty from a blank canvas – i.e. writing without preconceptions. There is much aesthetic merit to be found in this process. However, from a business perspective – i.e. if the number of books you sell has some importance to you – it may be worthwhile to consider the concept of your book first.

Will it Be Worthwhile to Publish Your Book?

How you determine whether or not it will be worthwhile to you to publish your book depends on how you measure your book's worth. If you care mostly about the artistic merit of your book, you should judge the aesthetic value of your work. If you care mostly about making something useful or entertaining available so that you can share it with others, you should measure how useful or entertaining your work is. But if you are more concerned with the royalties your book will draw, you should consider how well your book will sell.

The aesthetic worth of your book should mean more to you than anyone else. If you are pleased with your final product and you are almost entirely concerned with its artistic merit, you should be happy with your book regardless of the sales. If you wish to judge how it is artistically perceived by others, you can receive their feedback. Reviews can help convey this, too, though some reviews will focus on other aspects of your book, such as whether or not it is useful or entertaining.

If you are primarily aiming to write a book that is very useful, you should research the market first to see what other books are already available in the area you have in mind. Then you have to ask yourself if there is a need, which you can fill. If you don't have an area in mind, you can browse different types of books and try to find a need – thinking like an inventor: Look for a need, then try to fill that need. You also have to consider how well-suited you are to fill that need. If there are many experts in that area, and you are not an expert, that area might better be left to the experts. But sometimes amateurs can fill a need in ways that experts can't. Writing from the perspective of utility, you want your book to be useful, stand out from the competition, and be easy to find by your anticipated market. You can judge your book's usefulness from feedback and reviews.

Perhaps your primary goal is to entertain. There are many other books, in a variety of subjects, which aim to entertain in some way – not just comedy, but many works of fiction, and even nonfiction. You should consider what may make your book sell when there are so many forms of entertainment available, many of which are already popular and well-known. If you don't envision your book selling very well, ask yourself if entertaining a smaller audience may be sufficient for your needs. Again, entertainment is something you can judge from feedback and reviews.

But most of us have to pay the rent. If you want to write full-time, you definitely need to earn good royalties. If you're considering self-publishing, though, hopefully you already have a day job. Don't quit it unless and until at some point you become fortunate enough to have a steady income from your royalties that is good enough to do so. You probably already have your royalties spent even if you already have a full-time job – no matter what you make, you probably have several things in mind that you'd like to do with the revenue you make from sales of your book. (Don't forget that you'll have to pay taxes, and that the royalties will be reported to the IRS. Many people expect, incorrectly, that a 1099 will only be issued if the amount exceeds $600, but while $600 is the limit for many kinds of 1099's, the limit is just $10 for the reporting of royalties. If you receive $10 or more in royalties, you should get a 1099.)

So from the business perspective, you should consider the concept of your book and what its financial worth may be. If you haven't started writing yet, when you choose your concept, you will be better motivated if you have confidence that your concept will pay off to some degree financially. If you've already written your book, you may still want to consider whether any revisions may be worthwhile.

A good place to start is to research the competition. How to go about this is described in the next chapter. If you have a concept in mind, look for competing books with similar concepts. You can measure their success to some extent. You can also see how much competition there is. If you don't have a concept in mind, you can still browse available books in various subjects to help you develop your own concept. Researching what is already available on the market is a very useful tool available to writers.

Decide what aspects of the book are most meaningful to you: How will you measure the success of your book? To what extent are you interested in the aesthetic value, the usefulness, the entertainment value, or the royalties of your book? Then choose, or revise, the concept of your book with these criteria in mind.

Your goal of researching the competition that most closely matches your concept is to establish whether or not there may be enough demand for your book, in terms of what you want to get from your book – financially and otherwise. We'll return to the research issue in the next chapter, where you can get a better feel for how to estimate the potential success of your book.

Considering the Market for Your Concept

There are millions of ideas for books, and millions of books have been written. But not all book ideas are successful, including many that have been published. There are a lot of factors that may affect the success of a book idea, such as:
- writing about a popular subject (but see the next bullet, as these two are related).
- if there are already more books related to your idea than the market demands.
- how easy it is for your potential audience to find your book.
- how useful or entertaining your book is.
- if the book is well-organized and well-written.

- if the content is free of conceptual mistakes.
- what marketing strategies are employed.
- whether the cover attracts the target audience.
- if the content of the book fulfills what the cover, book description, and book reviews advertise.
- if readers appreciated the book enough to encourage family and friends to read it, too.

If you want your book to be successful, you need to consider the market for your book when you choose the concept and develop it more fully, and consider it again when you write and then revise your book.

Ask yourself who the target audience is – i.e. what groups of people are most likely to be interested in your book. How large is your audience? How will your audience learn about your book? (Not everyone searches for books on Amazon.com, of course. Amazon does have a very large audience, but many customers go to Amazon knowing specifically what they will buy, which means they've learned about the book they want before they visit the site.) How many other books are on the market for this audience? What distinguishes your book from the competition? Is it enough to drive sufficient sales? How willing are you to promote your own work?

It's important to consider the market for your book because you can't expect to sell copies to others if you don't first sell your concept to yourself. Also, identifying your intended audience is a necessary prelude to writing a book with that particular audience in mind.

> You need to sell your book to yourself before you can expect to sell it to others.

Once you have the main concept for your book and have ways in mind that will help to distinguish it from the competition, explore your concept more fully. Write a chapter outline if your book is nonfiction, or write a story outline if you are writing fiction. This will help you organize your thoughts and make sure that your idea is complete. It will probably force you to think about a few things that are missing or that you haven't yet thought through.

As your concept develops more fully, reassess the market for your book and its potential worth. Show your outline to family or friends for valuable feedback. Prepare yourself to accept constructive criticism, and realize that you are still free to decide whether or not to accept any advice. The feedback will provide some measure of how others may view your book. Your outline is a sketch of your vision for the book. Bear in mind that other people may look at your outline and see a different vision. Receiving feedback from your target audience, e.g. in a focus group, can be especially helpful. It may also be useful to join a writer's forum.

Once you are happy with the vision for your book and understand who you are writing the book for, you are ready to begin writing. Having thought the concept through and satisfied yourself that your book is worth writing, be ready to use this to motivate yourself to start and then continue writing. There will periods where your motivation dips or you question yourself or you get frustrated with the writing. When this happens, remind yourself that you thought this through already, and that you are confident that writing your book is worthwhile.

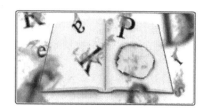

3 Researching the Competition

I T'S IMPORTANT TO identify books that are competitive titles, complementary titles, and otherwise related to the concept for your book. As you develop your book, this will help you see what is already on the market. Knowing what is presently available will help you to develop a book that is distinguished from the competition and fills one or more needs.

Complementary Books
Complementary titles serve as useful companions to one another, like a dictionary and thesaurus, which complement one another nicely.

Competitive Books
Competitive titles represent a choice that a reader has; once the reader selects one title, the reader will not have need of the others.

Part Competitive, Part Complementary
The definitions above are extreme; many related titles are not quite either. Most books are more complementary than they are competitive, since readers tend to buy many similar books and the "frequently also bought" lists tend to help the sales of both complementary and competitive titles.

Complementary titles are books that go well together – once a buyer has one, it will be useful to have the others. Once a few buyers buy your book and another book together, these other titles will show up on your book's product page, and your book may show up on the other books' product pages. Amazon encourages multiple sales (e.g. with free shipping on orders over $35), so when customers buy one book, they often browse related books. Complementary books often show up at the top of the page as "frequently bought together." So complementary, as well as competitive, titles affect the sales of your book.

If you are writing nonfiction, you will need to compile a list of references and cite related works. This provides one more reason for searching for competitive, complementary, and other related works.

Finding Related Works

Start out by visiting a couple of bookstores. Here, you can walk right up to shelves of books on your topic and find current books that the bookseller deemed popular enough to stock on their shelves. These books you can pick up and browse through. This will get you acquainted with a few related books. You don't need to spend an arm and a leg buying every related book you find; just get a feel for the market for now. You might carry a pocket notebook on which to write down the titles and authors, though, and perhaps jot down a few notes.

A major library will have some older books that bookstores likely will not have. Library books you can check out without putting a dent in your budget.

It's good to browse through physical copies of books, as you can learn quite a bit about them that way, but you won't find many of the books on the market at bookstores or libraries – so this won't complete your search. Remember to check the references at the back of these books, as many of these works may be related to your work.

Next, search online. Amazon has a large database of current and old, used and new books. First try browsing subjects, where you can find all of the books related to a single subcategory. Next try searching by a variety of keywords in books (not in specific categories, as some books will not appear in the categories you expect). Useful books will not always appear at the top of your search, so you'll want to spend some time browsing through search results. You can get ideas for other keywords to use by reading descriptions, covers, reviews, and contents of related books. Friends, family, and colleagues may suggest a few more keywords that you hadn't thought of.

Some online books will let you search inside – front and back cover, front matter, back matter, and contents. You can also see sample pages, but you won't be able to browse as much of the book as you can in a bookstore. When browsing through a physical book, you can see how many figures it has and how good they are, learn how technical the writing is, find out how well-written the book is, and several other aspects that may be of interest. Other online books will not have the Search Inside feature.

It will be useful to learn more about the online books, including those with no Search Inside. You might be able to find book reviews to offer some input, or you may be able to find physical copies of these books somewhere. If the cost is cheap and you're willing to invest, you might purchase a few of the books you find online that seem most useful. Remember, on Amazon you can recover some of your investment later by reselling these books used.

Compiling Your Research

For each book, you want to learn enough about it to decide if it's mostly competitive, mostly complementary, otherwise related, or not useful. Also note which seem most useful and relevant for your purposes.

These related works have much information that can be useful to you. For one, you want your own book to be distinguished from the competition, so you need to acquaint yourself with the market to achieve this. You really would like to learn what the market needs and supply this need. Browsing through related works may help you organize your ideas for your own work. You will also see a variety of styles and formatting – decisions you will need to make when you begin writing your own book. These titles will help you establish a fair price for your book.

Record notes now, which may prove to be useful later. List the books, indicate how they relate to your work (e.g. competitive or complementary), record the price and whether it is softcover, hardbound (since softcover generally sells for less), or an eBook, and make useful notes about each book – with more description for related works that you deem to be more useful to you. Separately, you may want to jot down ideas you get about your own book as you sort through the market.

You also want to measure the success of these books. Some may be bestsellers – this could be noted on the cover, on the book rack in a bookstore, on a description of the book, or on a bestseller list. If so, note this and consider why the book sold well. Was the author already well-known? Was the book promoted well? Was it distributed by a major publisher? Is it well-written? Does it fill a useful market need? Etc.

You can also gauge how well a book sells by searching for it on Amazon. Note that many books will have different editions available on Amazon, and some editions may sell better than others. If the book has sold on Amazon.com, it will have a sales rank on its webpage. (So if a book doesn't have a sales rank, it has yet to sell its first copy.)

Amazon.com Sales Rank

A book with a very low sales rank (like 5,000) sells with higher frequency, and a book with a very high sales rank (like 1,500,000) sells with very low frequency.

> The smaller the number of the Amazon.com sales rank, the better the book has been selling recently.

After a book has not sold for two or more days, the sales rank grows into the 200,000's and begins to climb. A book with a sales rank in the 1,000,000's has not sold for several days; some of the books with sales ranks in the millions may have not sold for a month or more.

For a book that has not sold for two or more days, if it suddenly sells on Amazon.com, shortly afterward the sales rank drops to about 100,000 and begins to climb back up. A book with a sales rank between 100,000 and 300,000 has probably sold within the last day or two. (The same concept applies to Kindle eBooks, but the numbers are somewhat different.)

In this way, the sales rank is more a measure of how long it has been since the book last sold. Since it can fluctuate considerably – being a very high number because it hasn't sold for several days, and then suddenly dropping down to a much lower number after a sale – it is not what you might intuitively expect. Sales rank combines sales data for the past day, week, and month.

Fortunately, the sales rank is not tied to the total number of copies that have sold on Amazon. This way, relatively new books can compete with popular books that have been on the market for a long period of time. If you do a search on Amazon that sorts results by best-selling, new books that have sold well recently can come up early in the search, and old books that have sold numerous copies but have been inactive recently will show up later in the search. This has a positive impact on your sales when you self-publish on Amazon, especially since your sales largely depend upon customers finding your book in a search. We'll discuss other ways that customers might find your book in a search in Chapter 10.

Books with sales ranks under 50,000 have probably sold two or more copies within the last day. A book with a sales rank under 10,000 has been selling well recently.

The sales rank can be deceiving, especially if you view the sales rank at a relative low or high for a particular book. However, if you monitor the sales rank over a period of time – like a couple of times a week for a few weeks – you can get a better measure.

If a book maintains a sales rank under 10,000 for a few weeks, it's a pretty hot seller. It is selling multiple copies every day.

If a book averages with a sales rank from 100,000 to 300,000 over a period of a few weeks, it is probably selling about a copy a day. A book that never drops below 1,000,000 probably has not sold at all while you've been monitoring its sales rank.

In addition to the sales rank, a book that is one of the top 100 sellers in a subcategory will give its rank, from 1 to 100, in that category. For example, a book that is #37 in sales in geometry is one of the top fifty sellers in the subcategory geometry. If instead it were #37 in mathematics, it would be an even better seller (since mathematics is a much broader category with numerous subcategories).

The sales ranks of related works can give you some idea of how well, or poorly, books like yours may sell on Amazon.com. This is important if you are trying to predict whether or not it may be financially worthwhile to write your book and self-publish it.

Bear in mind that many of the books that you find on Amazon also sell as physical copies in bookstores. Those books are selling more copies than Amazon's sales rank indicates.

If you intend to sell your books mostly on Amazon.com, then the sales rank is quite important to you as it will determine how often you receive royalties. If your book is only available on Amazon.com, then every copy you sell affects your book's sales rank. Note that there might be other books that sell reasonably well, but don't have a strong sales rank because only a fraction are sold through Amazon.

Ask yourself how many copies you expect to sell each month, and then try to determine if this is plausible. Browse the top sellers in the category that would be the best fit for your book. How often do these books sell on Amazon? This serves as an idea of the absolute best that you might expect.

You should also ask yourself what a reasonable expectation for your book is. Do you really have reason to expect your book to be a top seller? What is the competition in this category? Are the bestsellers written by popular authors or highly qualified authors? Are the bestsellers promoted well?

Try searching for books in your potential category that seem comparable to your book in some sense. Try searching for books published by CreateSpace to see how well these print-on-demand self-published books do in your category. This might serve as a better indication. Enter "CreateSpace Independent Publishing Platform" into the search field at Amazon.

Browse through the bestselling CreateSpace books at Amazon to see what types of books are selling well at the moment. Keep in mind that these stats can change considerably over the course of a month – a book that is selling very well today might not be selling well in a few weeks. Check out some of their sales ranks. Look for books that seem like they could be comparable to your book in some ways. Note that there are hundreds of thousands of books that are self-published on Amazon, but not all of these sell well. Also, there are thousands of books published with CreateSpace that use an imprint; many of these sell well, but won't show up in your search for CreateSpace books because they have an imprint name rather than CreateSpace listed under the publisher field at Amazon.

There are ways to help your sales grow once you make your book available. So whatever your sales rank is when your book starts out, it can improve over time. We'll look at marketing strategies, including some specific to Amazon.com, in Chapter 10. If you're concerned about how well your book will sell, you might browse through Chapter 10 now. If you're willing to implement some of these marketing strategies, you might develop some confidence that your book can be successful.

4 Preparing the Manuscript

I F YOU INTEND TO use CreateSpace to publish your book on Amazon.com, you will eventually need to create a PDF file, as described in Chapter 7. This is very common among self-publishing services. If you prepare your manuscript with Microsoft Word, you will be able to convert it to PDF later. Microsoft Word is convenient for most self-published authors because the most writers are familiar with this software and it is more economic than many specialized publishing programs, like Adobe InDesign, although Serif Page Plus is much more affordable. If you don't have access to Microsoft Word, consider Open Office.

In this book, I will provide formatting instructions for Microsoft Word 2003 and 2010 for Windows, as these are the most popular word processing programs used by self-published authors. Note that Microsoft Word 2007 and 2013 are very similar to 2010.

Before You Begin Writing

Collect and organize your thoughts into an outline. If you are writing nonfiction, prepare a chapter outline. First decide which topics to cover and in which order to present them. Next, give each chapter more detail: Either divide the chapters into sections or write a paragraph to describe what you will cover in each chapter. This will help you prepare a well-organized, structured, and complete manuscript. It will force you to think the concept for your book through, and the result will be a more detailed vision for your work.

For fiction, prepare a story outline, such as a summary of events. You might also develop some of your characters in advance by writing descriptions of them. This will help you stay organized as you write your story; you can refer to these notes to ensure that your book is self-consistent (posting your notes, character development, outlines, and related preparatory materials on your blog – see Chapter 10 – can help to build buzz for your coming book and can help develop a professional image). A few artistic writers of fiction like to write with a fresh canvas, so to speak – i.e. without any preconceptions. If this describes you, that's fine (some fiction authors strongly prefer it), but most of us benefit from organizing our ideas before we write.

Focus on writing your manuscript first, and save most of the formatting details for when your writing is finished. We'll discuss formatting in the next chapter, where the emphasis is on editing your manuscript. Much of the formatting requires more and more memory, so your computer is less likely to encounter problems if your document consists mostly of plain text as you write your manuscript.

Concentrate just on writing text. Don't worry about figures, tables, headings, footnotes, the title page, or any pages that require special formatting until the text is complete. Headings, footnotes, figures, and tables, for example, require more active memory just to open your document. Even if your computer has a lot of memory, you will be doing yourself a favor to save the formatting for later. If you want to draw pictures or create tables while they are fresh on your mind, make them in separate files – just one picture or table per file – to avoid memory-related problems.

> Save figures, tables, headings, footnotes, and all other formatting until after you complete writing the text in order to maximize the active memory of your computer while you type your manuscript. If you want to draw figures or create tables sooner, put them in separate individual files.

Save your file frequently. After you type a page of work, if you don't want to risk losing it, save it before writing more. Don't always save your manuscript with the same filename. I suggest including a version number with the filename, and updating the version regularly. For example, as you write the first chapter, you might save the file as Mystery 1.doc. Once you begin the second chapter, save it as Mystery 2.doc. You can have both chapters together in the same document. The idea is that if the most recent version of the file becomes corrupt, for example, you will have older versions to fall back on. Save your file in at least two different places, so that if you lose your file you still have another copy somewhere else. Unfortunately, computer problems are somewhat too common, but you can take measures to avoid losing your work. Save the file on a jump drive and also email it to yourself, for example.

> Save your manuscript regularly, and save it to two different places, like a jump drive and email. Change the version number frequently so that if you have problems with the most recent version, you can fall back on an older version.

Get a notebook or journal to carry around with you everywhere you go – such as a pocket notebook or journal that fits in a purse. You never know when you will think of a good idea for your book, so you want to be prepared to write it down whenever it comes. It's frustrating to remember that you had a good idea, but forgot exactly what it was. You might wake up at 2:00 a.m. with book ideas, so keep your notebook or journal near your bed, too.

> Be prepared to jot down book ideas whenever they may come. Keep a notebook or journal with you at all times.

Writing the Manuscript

To begin with, give some thought to writing a good title and subtitle. You want your title to be catchy, yet you want it to attract attention while still being informative – i.e. it should fit the genre or category well and convey something about your book. An optional subtitle can help you to elaborate on what your book is about.

Shorter titles tend to be more effective, especially in fiction. Shorter titles also have an advantage when it comes to marketing, as they are easier to remember and take up less room in online posts.

Nonfiction authors can include a few relevant keywords in the title and subtitle. However, it's more important for the title to read well and effectively convey the content; any keywords are secondary. If the title and subtitle are loaded with keywords, this strategy will probably backfire.

If you plan on selling largely through Amazon.com, including a couple of keywords that potential buyers may be searching for, which are related to your book, may help improve the visibility of your book in search results. Nonfiction authors can usually do this and still create effective titles; it's not as easy to squeeze keywords into fiction titles without making the title less effective (note that most bestselling fiction titles have just three words or less).

Keep in mind that you will have the opportunity to enter five keywords that aren't in the title or subtitle when you publish your book, so if there are relevant keywords that don't fit well in your title, you'll still have a chance to use them.

Give some thought to these keywords, and consider what keywords were useful when researching the competition for your book. You want your book to show up with searches of competitive and complementary titles, so you need to know what keywords are linked to those titles. You can't get every keyword into your title and subtitle, and it won't read well at all if your title is nothing but a jumble of keywords, so you will have to selectively identify just the most useful keywords. Once you submit your book for publishing, your title is fixed in stone, so choose it wisely. Consider feedback that you may receive from friends and family regarding your title. Focus on writing an effective title and subtitle. Keywords are secondary, and you get to add five keywords that aren't in your title or subtitle when you publish, so don't let keywords dictate your title for you. Remember, fiction titles usually don't have keywords; nonfiction titles usually use a few.

As you write your manuscript, bear in mind the importance of your book being well-written, well-organized, thorough, and self-consistent. You will receive reviews of your book once customers have bought your book and read it, and you want readers to recommend your book to their friends and family. So these details are important.

Invest in a book (or borrow one from a library) that describes rules of grammar and style. There are several such books, so you can easily find one that suits you.

You will also want a dictionary and thesaurus handy. You want readers to focus on the content of your book, but any time they come across a grammatical or spelling mistake, it will distract their attention. Many mistakes can be caught with a word processor such as Microsoft Word, but this process is not foolproof. For example, if you misspell a word that turns out to be a different word, this mistake will not be caught. For example, if you mean to write the word *spite,* but instead write the word *spire* – which is easy to do since these two letters are adjacent to one another on the keyboard – this mistake will not be caught by the computer.

A style manual will help your book read better. For example, it will remind you to think about the sentence structure, so that it is not too repetitive. You will also remember to avoid fragments and run-on sentences and a host of other details that can help you write better.

Many guides will also have word lists to help you mix things up. When you read your draft, look for repetitiveness. Your work will read better if the writing exhibits some variety. Word lists will include a variety of action verbs and descriptive adjectives, for example.

Decide whether to write in the first person, second person, or third person, and whether to use the singular or plural – i.e. using *I, me,* and *my;* or *we* and *our;* or *you* and *your;* or *he, she,* and *they.* There may be reasons to use more than one person – e.g. mostly *you* and *your,* but other times *I, me,* and *my.* This could be the case if you are writing a book to give advice to your audience, in which case *I* refers to the author and *you* the reader.

Also, choose a tense – past tense or present. For fiction, you will need to have a setting in mind, which may change in different scenes of your book.

Check out similar titles to see which person and tense they use. Use a search engine to find out which of these tend to appeal better to readers, which are easier to write, and which tend to be accepted in which genres.

Note that there are three popular conventions for dialog tags:

- Use a simple "he said" or "she said" to indicate who the speaker is. For example, John said, "My book is almost finished."
- Use a precise verb, with an adjective if helpful, when this helps to convey meaning or tone. For example, Martha whispered slowly, "The monster is right behind that door."
- Don't use any dialog tags when the speaker, tone, and meaning are clear from the context. For example: Roger bumped his head on the wall after slipping on Fred's roller skate. "Ouch! Fred, you're in big trouble, son."

Sometimes you will need to refer to page numbers, chapters, figures, or tables, or you will need to cite references. The page numbers you refer to can change frequently as you write and revise your book, and so can the numbers to chapters, figures, tables, and references. The best thing is to write ### or something else that will be easy to find later and save this for when your book is totally complete. When there is no longer a chance that these numbers may change, do a search on your word processor to find all instances of ### and then replace the ###'s with the appropriate numbers. Readers will be frustrated if you refer to incorrect chapters, pages, figures, tables, or references. Alternatively, you can use Word's built-in cross-reference tool.

Save referrals to page numbers, chapters, figures, tables, and references until your book is 100% complete in order to avoid referring to incorrect numbers.

There are a few different popular styles for how to cite references. Choose one that is appropriate for the type of book you are writing; look at some related works to develop a feel for this.

Plagiarism

Copying the work of another and passing it off as your own – even as little as a single phrase – is called plagiarism. Plagiarism is a very serious problem with serious legal consequences. Quote any sentences that you copy and properly cite the source(s) of your quotes or paraphrases, and stay within limits to how much you are permitted to cite, in order to avoid engaging in an instance of plagiarism.

Be sure to avoid plagiarism. If you copy one or more sentences, or even just a phrase, from another source, you must enclose this in quotation marks (") and cite the source as a reference – following the style guidelines for citing references. Even if you paraphrase the sentence, you need to cite your source. You also need to cite any research you may use to write your book. Failure to properly cite your reference for sentences that you copy or paraphrase can carry very serious legal consequences, so you definitely want to avoid this. There are limits to how much you can quote and paraphrase; an attorney can help you determine what constitutes "fair use."

Copying just one line from song lyrics can lead to legal action. Research "fair use" before quoting or paraphrasing anything for your book.

Note that citing your source does not relieve you of possible legal liabilities. Use a search engine to research "fair use." If you use just a single line from song lyrics, for example, the company that holds the rights to the lyrics can sue you for copyright infringement and even prevent the sale of your book until the issue is resolved.

Write with your intended audience in mind. Who is likely to read your book, and what will they be looking for? The answers to these questions affect how you should write your manuscript. For example, you need to consider at what level you should write, how much detail is appropriate, and what the reader will already know before picking up your book.

You want to make sure that you get your ideas across clearly and effectively. Consider the fact that different people think in different ways. If you ask a large group of people to describe how to eat an orange, you might be surprised by the results. Try it! Someone who thinks scientifically might describe this like a laboratory manual – starting with a technique for peeling the orange and finishing with putting the first bite in your mouth. Someone who thinks more passionately may instead describe how to enjoy the taste of the orange and savor the juices that shoot out when you bite down on it. It's important to consider how different people might interpret what you write. Being familiar with how your target audience thinks can help you out with this.

Some sections you will enjoy writing more than others. At some point, almost every writer gets frustrated. When this happens, you might take a little time off. Clear your mind and approach it when you feel fresh. The notion of completing a book can also feel overwhelming at times. The best way to deal with this is to force yourself to write one page at a time. Make a little progress here and there and this will add up – eventually, you will see that you are getting somewhere and this will lift your spirits. Look forward to the next part of the book that you will really enjoy, as this can help you with your motivation.

While you do want your writing to be very good, you're being too much of a perfectionist if you find yourself frequently deleting a large portion of your work and starting over. If this happens, you need to force yourself to write *something* and complete your work. Finish a draft of your work and you will gain a sense of completion. You can always go back and improve upon it afterward. It's important to feel that you are accomplishing something; it's better to finish a draft and then revise it than to spend too much time writing your first version.

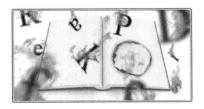

5 Editing and Formatting the Manuscript

ONCE YOUR BOOK IS complete, it is time to proofread your book for necessary revisions, add figures and tables, add front and back matter, and format your book interior, thereby transforming the design of your manuscript into a professionally formatted book interior.

CreateSpace has a variety of template Word documents (both blank and with sample formatted content) that you can use to prepare your manuscript with. Some authors find these helpful; some authors get frustrated trying to adjust the formatting.

The formatting prepared in the templates is minimal – it divides your document into sections for you. You gain much freedom starting with a blank Word document and formatting it yourself, and you can achieve everything the templates would do for you and much more without using them. Doing it yourself also spares you from having to figure out how to revise the formatting of the templates, add new sections, and adjust settings that might not appeal to you.

If you elect to use the templates, one thing you should do is change CreateSpace's pagination settings. In Word 2003, these are in Format > Paragraph > Line and Page Breaks; in Word 2010, go to the Home tab and click the funny icon in the bottom right corner of the Paragraph group, then choose the Line and Page Breaks tab. Uncheck Widow/Orphan Control, Keep With Next, Keep Lines Together, and Page Break Before (it's better to deal with these issues manually, as explained later in this chapter). You want to select all and apply these changes to the entire document (remove the blue dots from these checkboxes).

You have a choice between working with a .doc or .docx extension. If your book is mostly text, like a novel, the .doc extension will probably be simpler. Some rich formatting, such as the new equation tool (as opposed to the equation editor from 2003) is only supported in .docx format. If you use newer formatting features only available with .docx, you'll want to check how these features convert to PDF in Chapter 7. (You can make a test PDF now of the work that you've done so far.)

Revising Your Manuscript

When you finish writing the text, examine the content and organization. You will probably see some conceptual or organizational changes that you would like to make. These are the first types of revisions that you should attend to.

Next, you should proofread the text. Make sure that it reads well. Look for misspelled words, instances where you may have inadvertently used the wrong word, and grammatical mistakes. Also look for sentences or paragraphs that need more than just minor revisions. Rethink the content through as you read your manuscript. Check for content mistakes and self-consistency. Reconsider how the content is presented. Imagine yourself as a sample of your target audience reading the book for the first time, and highlight parts of the book that may be worth revising. Ask yourself if each part of the book reads well.

It is well worth having friends or family read your manuscript. Prepare yourself for some constructive criticism, then ask for honest constructive comments – what they like and what they don't. Consider their ideas, comments, and suggestions, as this is a sample of what readers may notice and think when they read your book. Ultimately, you have to judge whether or not to make revisions based on one or more of these suggested revisions; not all of them will be for the best. Everyone will have a different vision for what your book could be. It is your writing, so you are responsible for making these decisions, but many people (hopefully!) will be reading it, so your decisions will impact them (and perhaps how many people read your book).

Focus your attention on the basic text first. Once that is done, then move onto other aspects of your book.

Figures, Tables, and Equations

Note: You might want to add headers, footnotes, and page numbers prior to adding figures, tables, and equations. Otherwise, the placement of figures, tables, and equations may shift after adding these formatting features. See the last section in this chapter for information about headers and page numbers.

Before you add figures, tables, and equations to your manuscript, save your plain text document. Then resave it with a different filename – like MystFig1.doc instead of MystPlain4.doc. This way, if you experience any problems with your file after adding figures, tables, and equations, you will still have your plain text file to fall back on. Remember to save your files with different version numbers, so if after adding the tenth figure you have a file problem, you may still be able to open a version that has some of the figures. Also save your files in more than one place – like on a jump drive and email it to yourself, just in case (too safe is better than sorry).

Let me remind you that I will focus on how to use Microsoft Word 2003 and 2010 for Window in this book, since most self-published authors use one of these programs (2007 and 2013 are very similar to 2010). Some of these techniques can also be applied to other programs, but it's not feasible for me to try to explain how to use every software package on the market.

Photographs and other pictures that you have already saved in individual files can be inserted into your manuscript. In Microsoft Word, go to the Insert tab and choose Picture. Once you insert your picture, you can right-click on it and choose from an assortment of options. If you simply left-click on the picture once, you will be able to access a toolbar for formatting the picture. Some of the basic options include cropping and resizing (lock the aspect ratio first). However, it's better to crop and resize the picture in the native picture program and not adjust it after inserting the image into your Word file, otherwise the picture may print with less than its maximum resolution (see Chapter 6).

I strongly recommend choosing a wrapping style that is in line with the text, which you can find under Layout after you right-click on the picture (and choose Format Picture). Other types of layouts require much more of your computer's active memory, which slows your system down and makes it much more susceptible to serious problems – like the file closing while you are working on it or becoming corrupt. With the picture wrapped in line with the text, you can simply click the centering icon in order to center the picture.

When you can format a picture to be in line with the text, this helps minimize memory and other problems.

If you want a picture to appear centered horizontally and placed on its own line (or its own page), adjust the layout to be in line with text. If you want the paragraph to wrap around the image, use square or tight wrapping instead (but note that the positioning can change as you edit the document). Depending on your needs, placing the picture in front of or behind text may be the best option: This takes more memory, which may be an issue if you have numerous pictures (in which case it might help to separate your file into smaller documents).

You can draw black-and-white as well as color pictures that appear very professional in Microsoft Word. Once you acquaint yourself with the basic drawing tools, as described in the next chapter, you should see that you have much more flexibility in drawing than you might expect. Every diagram in my books on extra dimensions was drawn using Microsoft Word and/or Microsoft Excel. All of the covers for my books, including those that feature drawings of golf holes, were drawn in Microsoft Word (except for the cover of this book and *Spooky Word Scrambles*, which were designed by artist Melissa Stevens at www.theillustratedauthor.net). Every picture was drawn from scratch using basic drawing tools – there was no clipart or copying and pasting of other pictures (except for pictures that I had already drawn myself, and where I needed another picture like it). If you browse through the covers of my books (you can find them easily on Amazon), you will see a sample of the drawing possibilities offered by Microsoft Word. (The two exceptions include the covers for this book and *Spooky Word Scrambles*.)

I have used specialty drawing programs in the past, like Corel Draw, yet Microsoft Word is fairly good. It's also very convenient if you type your text in Microsoft Word and plan to have your completed manuscript in Microsoft Word, too. Some people like Paint, but I find that pictures drawn in Paint often come out looking very unprofessional on the screen as well as in print (e.g. edges often appear jagged and if you look closely, you may see stray marks). If you explore the drawing tools that I describe below for Microsoft Word, you will be able to make illustrations that look more professional.

However, if you have access to PhotoShop and have some expertise with it, you can create some highly professional pictures with that. More than just having the software, you want to have some experience with Photo-Shop and a good understanding of the graphic arts techniques that it entails (in order to avoid common design mistakes made with filters and layers, for example).

Regardless of how you make your diagrams, you should save your figures in separate files. So even if you use Microsoft Word to draw your figures, start with a blank document and save them in individual files. That way, if the interior file with both text and figures becomes corrupt, you may still be able to retrieve the figures individually. Save your figures separately, save your text file by itself, and once all are complete, save yet a new file with both text and figures together.

If you draw diagrams in Microsoft Word, once a diagram is complete, select all of the objects in your drawing and group the objects together to create a single drawing. Where viable, right-click the image to change the layout to be in line with the text. Again, this will help to conserve memory and avoid problems.

> Consult the next chapter for instructions on how to use Microsoft Word's drawing tools.

If you use another program to draw a picture, make a graph, or make a photo, after inserting this picture into Microsoft Word, you can still use Microsoft Word's drawing tools to add to the picture. You can also add textboxes to create labels. Use basic textboxes. Right-click textboxes, then choose no outline and no fill for the outline and fill colors – since diagrams look more professional when the labels aren't surrounded by rectangles, and if the fill is instead white the label will block out part of the picture.

> Change the outline color from black to no outline to make textboxes look like professional labels. Similarly, change the fill color to no fill so that the labels do not block any parts of the pictures.

Note that if you crop, resize, or otherwise edit imported pictures in the Word document, the images may get compressed. Ideally, you want your images to be 300 DPI. Some images look fine at 200 or 150 DPI, while others look noticeably better at 300 DPI. Word has a tendency to compress images such that they print at 200 DPI or less. You must take steps to avoid this compression, as described in Chapter 6.

In older versions of Microsoft Word (2003 and prior), you may be able to group imported pictures, textboxes, and drawing elements that you create in Microsoft Word together into a single object (but see the note in the previous paragraph). Then you can right-click this single object to change the layout to be in line with the text. Some of the newer versions of Word may restrict what can or can't be grouped together. If possible, avoid having many images floating around your document that are not in line with the text as this leads to memory and file problems.

If you have a large number of tables, figures, and/or equations, I recommend separating your book into several files – one file per chapter. This makes the file size more manageable and frees up active memory so that your programs work faster and are less susceptible to problems. When each chapter is complete, you can copy and paste them all into one large document (or, better yet, if you have a PDF converter that allows you to join separate PDF files together, you can simply leave your Word files separate).

You can draw tables in Microsoft Word by going to Insert and choosing Table (or in older versions going directly to the Table tab). When your cursor is in the table, you will be able to access design and formatting features as well as table tools. Table properties let you change the width and height of cells, rows, columns, or the whole table, modify text position, and more. You can easily add or remove rows or columns, split cells, merge cells, and so on. The tools are very intuitive. It just takes a little exploration to get used to where to find the features you are looking for. Remember that Microsoft Word has a Help feature to help you figure out what you need. In the worst case, you can probably find someone to ask for a little help.

You may want to type a numbered caption beneath each figure and table. If so, prepare these meticulously: Make sure that you follow the exact same format each time, otherwise the alert reader may be distracted by non-uniformity. If you plan to describe the tables and figures in the text, numbering them can help the reader find the tables and figures that you refer to. This is particularly useful if the tables and figures that you describe are not near the text that refers to them – for example, if you refer to a figure in Chapter 3 when you are writing Chapter 7. Some books do not have table and figure captions, though. It's partly a matter of function and partly a matter of style.

If you use any math in your book you will need to include equations. Microsoft Word has a built-in tool for creating equations, which is pretty intuitive. If you are writing a mathematical or scientific book that will involve regular use of equations, you might prefer Microsoft Word 2007 or later, as the newer equation tool has many improved formatting possibilities compared to the 2003 equation editor. You must save the file as .docx, not .doc, in order to use the new equation tool. (Find the new equation editor in Insert > Equation; find the old editor in Insert > Object > Microsoft Equation 3.0. In Word 2007 and up, you must use the old editor in .doc mode, but can use the new editor in .docx mode.)

If you have extensive use of equations, an alternative is obtaining, learning, and using LaTeX – which lets you write equation commands in a basic text editor, which transform into formatted equations when a compiler converts your text file to PDF.

If you type equations, following are some conventions that you should be aware of. Symbols that represent constants (e.g. the speed of light c) and variables (e.g. position x) should appear italicized (the default setting in Microsoft Word's equation editor), but units (like m/s) should not be italicized (you will need to change these to normal). Vectors should appear in boldface and/or have an arrow over them (like $\vec{\mathbf{A}}$). Browse through various mathematics textbooks and papers for more style choices.

If you need to add an equation to a diagram – perhaps creating a mathematical label – in Microsoft Word 2003 you can right-click the equation and change the layout to be in front of text. In Microsoft Word 2007 and up, you can first insert a plain textbox (removing its outline and fill) and then insert an equation into the textbox (or, if the equation is already typed, cut and paste the equation into the textbox). Afterward, remember to group objects together and to make the group in line with the text, whenever this is viable.

Front and Back Matter

Front and back matter are sections that appear at the beginning or end of the book. Front matter commonly includes the title page, copyright page, table of contents, and one or more of the following: introduction, prelude, dedications, and acknowledgements. Acknowledgments may also appear at the end of the introduction instead of in a separate section. Back matter commonly includes one or more of the following sections: appendices, references (or bibliography), glossary, index, about the author, and advertisements for other books. Trying to include all of these sections is overkill. Choose those that are most relevant for your work.

Almost all books begin with a title page, which has a copyright page on its back side. The title page should include the title, subtitle, and author, and may have other information and even figures; it could simply be a black-and-white copy of the front cover (unless you are writing a book with a color interior). The title page should be centered both horizontally and vertically. To center it vertically, highlight the text and go to Page Layout, where you can choose to vertically center only the highlighted text (not the section or entire document). After, check the page(s) that follow to see that they didn't get vertically centered, too. It might help to temporarily add an extra blank line to the end of the title page and highlight only the text preceding this line before centering vertically. Sometimes a new blank page will appear after, which you will have to delete – with trial and error you can delete any blank pages without undoing the vertical centering.

Including a copyright page will make your book appear more professional. The copyright page should include the title and subtitle, but in a smaller size font – whereas the title page should use a larger font for the title – and the author's name. Indicate the year after a copyright symbol, like © 2009. You may want to include a note about the rights being reserved and that no portion of the book may be copied in any form without the author's permission. You should write this in your own words to avoid plagiarism. (However, you have permission to copy and use the copyright note that I used on the copyright page of my book – or modify it as you see fit.) Most fictional works also include a statement to the effect that all persons and places are purely fictional and that any resemblance to real people or places is purely coincidental. Of course, an attorney can advise you best.

Examine traditionally published books similar to yours and study their copyright pages, title pages, front matter, back matter, headers, footers, layout, design, font styles, indentation sizes, justification or centering, vertical justification or centering, and so on. These models can help you perfect the design of your book.

> Find books similar to yours in libraries and bookstores (also explore Look Insides at Amazon) and study their front matter, back matter, headers, footers, and other formatting, layout, and design features. Use these as guides for the formatting of your book (but don't plagiarize their designs).

A copyright page may also indicate the category for your book. You should include the ISBN number on the copyright page. You don't know this yet (unless you happen to already have one), so save this until you are ready to submit your files for publishing. Once you set up your account to load your files, you will receive an ISBN-10 and EAN-13, which you can simply copy and paste into your copyright page before making your final PDF files. Publishers also indicate the edition number and a series of numbers for the print number. You can include an edition number, optionally, but those printing numbers don't make sense for print-on-demand. Study traditionally published copyright pages to find other ideas, like including the category.

I suggest inserting a table in Microsoft Word with two columns and several rows for your table of contents. Move the column divider far to the right – just enough to type a three-digit number like 256 (try this to check that it's wide enough). You can change the formatting of the table so that it doesn't show the cell borders (actually, it will turn these gray in color so that you can see them on the screen, but the borders won't print – well, you should check this to be sure). Alternative to the table, you can make two uneven columns of text (by changing the format to two columns). There is also a Table of Contents tool under References.

The other front matter and back matter sections are straightforward to make – they mostly consist of text. Basically, you just need to look at some samples from traditionally published books to develop an idea for how these should read and appear.

Formatting Your Manuscript

It's good to save the formatting for last. Doing all the formatting in a short period of time helps to have a uniformly formatted book – otherwise you might forget what choices you have made and format parts of the book differently. The placement of figures, tables, and equations is sensitive to the structure of your document. That is, if you insert a figure prematurely and later add or remove text before the figure, the figure will appear in a different place – perhaps partway between two pages. So it's best to wait until the text is completed, then insert figures, tables, and equations exactly where you want them to appear. Subtle formatting like manual hyphenation, widows, orphans, and kerning can't be implemented until the pages are otherwise finalized – you have to redo these features every time you make any revisions to the text or page layout.

Examples of Justified Text

This paragraph is aligned left. This paragraph is aligned left. This paragraph is aligned left. This paragraph is aligned left. This paragraph is aligned left. This paragraph is aligned left. This paragraph is aligned left. This paragraph is aligned left.

This paragraph is aligned right. This paragraph is aligned right. This paragraph is aligned right. This paragraph is aligned right. This paragraph is aligned right. This paragraph is aligned right. This paragraph is aligned right. This paragraph is aligned right.

This paragraph is centered.
This paragraph is centered.
This paragraph is centered.
This paragraph is centered.
This paragraph is centered.

This paragraph is justified full. This paragraph is justified full. This paragraph is justified full. This paragraph is justified full. This paragraph is justified full. This paragraph is justified full. This paragraph is justified full. This paragraph is justified full.

For most books, the body text should generally be justified full – that is, both the right and left edges of the text should appear to line up very nicely. Contrast this with left alignment (also called ragged right), right alignment (ragged left), or centered. Chapter headings, figures, tables, equations, and notes that you want to stand out might be centered on their own lines. The copyright page and a few other pages might be aligned left (or centered) instead of justified full.

Microsoft Word lets you justify, align, or center text easily by clicking an icon that mimics the structure of the text. First highlight the text you wish to justify, align, or center, then click the icon.

Many new authors don't like the gaps they see with fully justified text, but if you think about it, the gaps at the right edges of left-aligned text are even bigger. This is why left alignment is often termed ragged right. Since almost all traditionally published books are justified full, if your book is aligned left, it may have a self-published look to it.

Here is a tip: Use hyphenation with your fully justified text. This will reduce the gaps in many cases. You can do this manually (but consult a dictionary first), or you can turn on Word's hyphenation tool to do this automatically. Don't do any manual hyphenation until your text and page layout are perfected, otherwise you'll get stray hyphens mid-line.

Use full justification and hyphenation for a more professional appearance.

In Word 2003, look for Tools > Language > Hyphenation. In Word 2010, look for Page Layout > Hyphenation; also, go to File > Options (below Help) > Advanced > Layout Options (at the bottom) and check the box to hyphenate like WordPerfect for improved hyphenation. Increase the hyphenation zone to about

0.4, otherwise you get an excessive number of hyphens. You might also wish to limit the number of consecutive hyphens. To undo an automatic hyphen, place the cursor at the beginning of the word and press Shift + Enter. With automatic hyphenation turned on, you can still insert hyphens manually, if desired (but once you insert manual hyphens, any revisions you make to your document may cause those hyphens to appear mid-line instead of at the end of the line where you inserted them, so you must watch out for this possibility).

Another way to reduce the gaps in fully justified text is to use a single space after the period, instead of two. Many well-educated people believe that you're supposed to use two spaces after a period, but this rule actually applies to using a typewriter, not publishing books. If you study the typeset of traditionally published books carefully, you can actually see that it's "correct" to only use one space after the period. This practice also spreads the spaces out better for fully justified text. If you already have two spaces after your periods, you just need to use the Replace tool to fix this quickly. If you doubt that one space is correct, I encourage you to Google a fascinating article called "Space Invaders" in *Slate Magazine* by Farhad Manjoo.

> When publishing a book, it's correct to use one space after a period, not two.

You'll want to note the distinction between hyphens (-) and dashes (– or —); dashes are longer. Use hyphens in hyphenated words (like good-hearted), to create hyphenated adjectives (like red-haired, blue-eyed girl), or to hyphenate a word that would otherwise go onto the next line, leaving large gaps in the previous line of justified text (like the word "justified" in this sentence). In contrast, dashes are used as separators – like this—or like this; they help to separate phrases that interrupt the main flow of the text.

The hyphen (-) appears on your keyboard. In Microsoft Word, you can create a dash automatically by typing a space, hyphen, then space or two consecutive hyphens (--) if the AutoCorrect feature is enabled. A better way (if you might make an eBook, this method is better at preserving these symbols) is to hold down the Alt key and type 0150 or 0151 to create the short (–) and long (—) dashes, respectively called en and em dashes. Include spaces around the short dash – like this – but not around the long dash—like this. Choose either the short or long dash and be consistent throughout your book; don't use both as I've done in this paragraph.

The long dash can also be used to set off a quotation (in this case, with a space), as in the example below.

> Better to write for yourself and have no public, than to write for the public and have no self. — Cyril Connolly in *The New Statesman*

Choose the style and size of your font. Times New Roman 12-point font is particularly common for the body of the text, but some people view Times New Roman as amateurish because it's used in many self-published books. This book utilizes Georgia, which is a little bolder than Times New Roman (the fact that Georgia looks similar to Times New Roman may be a drawback); another common choice for fiction is Garamond (it's somewhat lighter, though some readers feel it may be too light). It's worth researching fonts and choosing wisely for your unique book. For most common fonts, 10 to 12 points is a good place to start: The best test is to print out a sample page and compare it with traditionally published books serving as your models (don't make an exact replica, though – just use these models to guide your own ideas). The title, subtitle, chapter, and section headings often use a larger font size or appear in boldface (or both).

When you convert your book to PDF format for publishing, you'll need to embed the fonts. If you're not using one of Word's preinstalled fonts, you'll want to check that it allows commercial use and that it can be embedded in the PDF file. When you download a font or buy a font package, check the font license and see if commercial use is permitted. If so, once you download the font, find the font file (it may be in the fonts folder in the Control Panel or a location that you specified when you saved it; if not, try searching for it by name on your computer), right-click the font file, click Properties and Details, and look under Embeddability. If it says "No embedding permissions," you won't be able to embed the font in the PDF file. If it can be embedded, this doesn't guarantee that the font can be used for commercial use, so you must also check the font license. Check Font Squirrel and Font Space online for a selection of fonts to choose from. However, sticking to a common font like Georgia or Garamond may make your book more readable. At the very least, search online to find opinions on a font before adopting it.

You want your readers to be able to read your book without too much eye strain, but the larger the font size, the more pages your book will have and therefore the more your book will cost. In Times New Roman, Calibri, Georgia, Garamond, and many common fonts, the 12-point size is quite readable for most people. If your book is very long, you can save pages with a 10-point font, which is sometimes used. Publishers sometimes offer large print books with larger font sizes, for books popular enough to print a special edition for readers who require a larger font size. Some font styles often appear larger or smaller than other fonts of the same point measure; you can type a sentence in a variety of font styles and print the page as a means of comparison.

The default indent size in Microsoft Word is 0.5", but many traditionally published books use a smaller size, especially for books with smaller page sizes. You can measure the indents of traditionally published books similar to yours to see what's common. Don't use the spacebar to create tabs. If you'll be making an eBook version, too, don't use the tab key (or you'll wind up with crazy formatting for your eBook). Instead, use the First Line option in the Paragraph dialog box (in Word 2010, click the funny icon in the bottom right corner of the Paragraph group on the Home tab; in Word 2003 look on the Format menu): Change Special to First Line and manually set the numerical measure to properly indent a paragraph. You don't have to do this manually to every paragraph though: You can use the Styles feature built into Word. Right-click on the Normal style (at the top of the Home tab in Word 2010, or on the Formatting toolbar of Word 2003), choose Modify Style, click Format, select Paragraph, and set First Line. (You may also need to adjust other properties of the style, such as font style and size: The easy way to do this is to highlight a paragraph with the style set the way you like it, right-click on Normal style, and click Update. Then adjust the First Line in Normal style.) Once the Style is modified, it's easy to "paint" formatting.

Another issue is the leading. Basically, this determines the space between lines. Professional designers are familiar with measures specified in terms of font points (or relative to the em). If you don't want to get technical, the practical method is to play with the line-spacing, print out sample pages, and compare with traditionally published books to get this right.

There are two common ways to create section breaks: Use three asterisks between two blank lines (like the one below) or use consecutive blank lines. Some traditionally published books indent the beginning paragraph of the subsequent section, others don't. Explore books that are similar to yours to see what's common (that's what readers will be accustomed to).

* * *

Go to Page Layout to choose the size of your pages. First go to the publisher's website (e.g. CreateSpace) to see what trim sizes are available for your book. Note that there are restrictions on the number of pages permitted for your book based on the trim size and whether the interior is black-and-white or color – so make sure that the page count doesn't exceed the limits for the trim size that you select. In Page Layout, choose to apply this to the entire document (otherwise, you might only change the page size for one section) and set the page size to match the desired trim size.

Determine the sizes of some related books to help you choose a suitable trim size. The 5.5" x 8" trim size is close to mass market size. Trade paperback is somewhat larger. Note that it will be challenging to compete with mass market pricing, so marketing your book as a trade paperback may have an advantage. At CreateSpace, a larger trim size costs the same as a smaller trim size – but the larger trim size means fewer pages, which will reduce the cost of your book (unless it has fewer than about a hundred pages for black-and-white or forty pages for color, in which case page count doesn't affect price). So you don't actually save money with a smaller size book; rather, this might cost you more money.

Set the page margins in Page Layout. I recommend .5" for the left, right, top, and bottom margins, plus a

0.5" gutter (what Word calls a gutter is really a half-gutter). Alternatively, if you adjust the setting of Multiple Pages, the options will include inside and outside margins instead of left and right: In this case, choosing 1" for the inside margin, 0.5" for the outside margin, 0.5" for the top and bottom, and 0" for the gutter will be equivalent. But before implementing my suggestion, first check to see what's common in your genre. Also, if you need to reduce your page count, one thing to consider is adopting narrower margins. Be sure to meet the minimum inside and outside margins that CreateSpace specifies: 0.25" outside margins, and an inside margin of 0.375" for up to 150 pages, 0.75" for up to 400 pages, 0.875" for up to 600 pages, and 1" for more pages.

In Page Layout, choose different odd and even pages, and different first page, too. The gutter is an extra 0.5" width (it's only 0.5" in my example – it may be different for your book) added to the right or left margins: If you check the box to have different formatting on odd and even pages, then the gutter will automatically place the 0.5" on alternate sides of odd and even pages to leave an extra 0.5" on the edge of the page that fits into the binding of the book. I highly recommend this. (Again, if you work with inside and outside margins instead of left and right, then just make the inside margin larger – it would be 1" in my example – and set the gutter to zero.)

Insert page numbers and browse through the options for style and numbering. I like to choose a basic style that has the page number positioned where I would like it, and then format the page numbering after inserting it. Note that you can type symbols before and after the page number, like ~ 4 ~ instead of just 4. You can choose the page numbers to show on the outside or inside – meaning that it will alternate position on the left and right sides of the pages to always show up at the outside or inside edge of the page. Alternatively, page numbers can be centered. Also, page numbers can appear at the top or bottom of the pages.

Most books also have page headers (not to be confused with headings – a header appears at the top of nearly every page, whereas a heading precedes a chapter or section). You probably want different headers for odd and even pages. You might put the title on odd-page headers and your name on even-page headers, for example. I like to enter a linespace after the title or name, select the header text and linespace, go to format paragraph, switch from text to paragraph, and insert a horizontal line in the middle of the paragraph (all this while in the page header) – that's how I created the header that appears at the top of the pages of the paperback edition of this book. But browse other books and play around with this to see what suits you best.

Another common option is to put chapter names on the even pages and the title of the book on odd pages. There is a trick to doing this with Microsoft Word. The same trick is used to omit the page numbers from the first few pages, use Roman numerals for front matter, use Arabic numbers for most pages, and omit page numbers from the first page of each chapter. The trick has to do with creating sections. Backup your file and save it with two different filenames before you play with the headers and footers: Sometimes the file becomes corrupt, and if it does you'll be happy if you have another copy of your file saved somewhere (save it in a couple of places, like jump drive and email, just in case).

To use different kinds of page numbers (e.g. Roman numerals, Arabic numbers, and no numbers on selected pages) or different kinds of headers in different parts of your book, you must use section breaks. You want to divide your file up into sections where each "section" is a part of your book that will use a different style of page number or header. Remember to look at traditionally published books similar to yours as a guide for page numbering and header options.

Most books have no page numbers until the introduction, in which case the second "section" would start at the introduction. Then page numbering typically switches from Roman numerals to Arabic numbers in Chapter 1, which would begin a new section. If you want each chapter to have its name on the even-page headers, you must begin a new section with each chapter. You'll also need to decide how to separate your back matter into sections.

When a new "section" (as I've just defined it) needs to begin, remove the page break beginning the section and insert a Next Page break under Breaks in Page Layout instead. Don't use an ordinary page break because that won't define where a new section needs to start; the Next Page feature tells Microsoft Word where the page numbering or header style needs to change.

Next, start at the beginning of the document and systematically go through – section by section – and insert and adjust the page header and numbering options. When you place your cursor in the header of footer area, uncheck the box that says to link to the previous section until the Same as Previous flag disappears; then you can modify the current section's header or footer without messing up the previous section. After you change a section, go back to the previous section and make sure it's still okay. Occasionally, Word gets fussy and you need to use the Undo button, remove the current page break, insert a new Next Page section break, and try again.

The first page of a chapter often doesn't start at the top of a page. You can use the Enter key to drop it down a few lines, or you may find it more reliable to go into the Paragraph dialog box and enter a numerical measure for how far it should drop down. The chapter heading usually has a larger font style. The first letter often has a drop cap (Word has a built-in tool for this), and the first few words may also APPEAR IN CAPS.

Headers and footers can serve a function by providing valuable information (like page numbers and chapter names). They can also include a design that fits the theme of the book well. One other thing that they may do, which can be a problem, is distract the reader from the main text.

Most traditionally published books avoid widows. A widow is a single line of a paragraph that winds up on a page separated from the rest of the paragraph. You could revise the text to deal with widows, but ideally you would first perfect the text and design the page layout around the content, not revise the wording to fit the layout. There are a variety of methods to deal with widows, such as adding or removing hyphenation in end-of-line words, adjusting the kerning (look for the Advanced features in the Font dialog box), adding a tiny indent to either side of a paragraph, or making a slight adjustment to font size in one paragraph. The goal is to create an effect that the reader won't notice (like an indentation so small you can't see it with your eye unless you know to look for it) that eliminates the widow. Don't worry about widows until your content is otherwise perfected, otherwise you'll have to undo and redo these changes every time you revise the text or layout. Perfect and proofread your book carefully before worrying about widows.

In addition to eliminating widows, every page of the book lines up at the top and bottom (set the Vertical Alignment to Top in Page Layout) in most traditionally published books. This is especially important for novels and books that consist mostly of text. Some pages, like those with chapter or section headings, might not align at the bottom with the rest unless you play with the space before or after paragraphs for the heading text or make some other tiny adjustment to the paragraphs.

When you finish adding in all the figures and complete the formatting, scan through your document to see how all this formatting may have affected your book. You'll probably find extra or missing linespaces, strange page breaks, and other odd formatting features. You definitely don't want to publish your book without finding and correcting all of the formatting problems.

Proofread your book thoroughly. Receive feedback from friends and family. Make all of the final changes. Then put in the references to chapter numbers, page numbers, figures, tables, equations, and sources cited. If you wrote these as ### earlier, search for ### (using the Find option) and change all of these ###'s to the appropriate numerical values.

Now you should check that these changes didn't affect the formatting, and double-check these cross-references. Then your book interior will be complete – except for adding the ISBN and EAN to the copyright page, which you can do before making your PDF file and after setting up your account with CreateSpace (who can supply you with an ISBN before you upload your files).

If you have to make more changes for some reason, you'll want to check the formatting and cross-references carefully to make sure that these changes didn't cause more problems than they were worth. You can make changes even after your book is published and you start selling copies, but you want the quality of your book to be excellent when the first copy sells because the first customer could leave you a review that affects your sales for the life of your book. It affects not only the book, but your reputation as an author. We all make mistakes (if we're human), so if you find one, don't sweat it. Just do your best to keep the mistakes to a minimum.

Making an eBook

Don't accept CreateSpace's offer to send your file to Kindle. The reason is that PDF files almost never format well as eBooks. If you don't want your Kindle eBook to suffer from many formatting problems (even though it may look wonderful as a PDF file, it probably won't look good on Kindle without reformatting), you need to convert your Word document for proper Kindle formatting yourself. Simply ignore CreateSpace's offer to transfer your files to Kindle.

Make a new version of your Word document for Kindle. You should have two files for your book – one for your paperback and a separate file for your eBook.

Remove the following features from your paperback book file because they don't apply to eBooks:

- Remove headers, footers, page numbers, borders, bullets (the new Kindle supports bullets, but not perfectly – you should test them out across all devices before adopting them), and references to pages (like "see p. 42," which you can change to "see Sec. 5.2," for example).
- Remove the page numbers from your table of contents. Format your table of contents as a single-column list for now. (Later, you will add bookmark hyperlinks to it.)
- Remove the index if you have one, since there are no page numbers (and it's not really necessary, since eReaders have a search function).
- Remove any instances of two or more consecutive line breaks (made by pressing Enter).
- Remove any tabs. (If you used the spacebar to create indents, you need to remove those spaces.) You will need to make indents with the First Line method (to be described later) instead in order to avoid inconsistent and automatic indenting.

- Change multi-column text to a single column.
- Remove any text from textboxes and paste it into the main document.
- Remove any drop caps. A better alternative is to just type the first few words of the chapter in CAPS. Kindle supports drop caps, but they won't look perfect across all devices; you can also just change the first letter to a large font size, but that has problems, too.
- Remove any instances of two or more consecutive spaces (i.e. made using the spacebar). Even after a period, you want only one space, not two (otherwise, when a period happens to come at the end of a line, an extra space will appear at the end of the line and it won't look like the book was justified correctly).
- Remove tables. The new Kindle version is supposed to support simple tables, but you should first test this out in a preview on all devices to see how they look. You can make a table into a picture, but details may not show on a small screen.
- Some eReaders may not support footnotes or endnotes. Kindle supports basic endnotes that function as bookmark hyperlinks (not displaying on the "page," of course). As with your entire book, you should preview it on every device to see how it looks and works before publishing.
- Remove any fancy text effects (i.e. fancier than underlining, boldface, and strikethrough) – like glow or WordArt (you can format these as pictures instead, if they are legible on small screens and if it's done in moderation).
- Page breaks that are removed and replaced with Page Layout > Breaks > Next Page section breaks may format better on a couple of devices.

Even though indents may look perfect on your screen when you're using Microsoft Word, they might appear much different on a Kindle device. That's because eReaders treat indents much differently. If you use the tab key or spacebar to create indents, your eBook will probably suffer big problems with indents.

To create indents properly for eBook formatting, you must go into the paragraph dialog box (in Word 2010, click the funny icon in the bottom right corner of the Paragraph group on the Home tab; in Word 2003, look on the Format menu), go to Special, choose First Line, and set the value. It's common to use 0.2" to 0.3" for eBooks (because 0.5" would be large on an iPhone).

Don't do this paragraph by paragraph. Use the Style feature built into Word. You need to use the Styles to achieve proper eBook formatting in Word for more reasons than just indents. Ultimately, eBooks work like HTML files and the Styles feature helps translate your Word file to an eBook file properly.

You need to make at least four different Styles: one for body text with indents, one for non-indented paragraphs or lines, one for headings, and one for titles. You might name these styles Normal, FirstNormal, Heading 1, and Title (that's what I will call them in what follows):

- Apply the Normal Style to most of your document. This Style will create an indent using First Line (click Format when modifying the Style to get into the paragraph settings).

- For any non-centered paragraphs or lines (like the first paragraph of a chapter, subheadings, or lines from your copyright page) that you don't want automatically indented, apply the First-Normal Style. For this Style, you must set the indent to 0.01". **Unfortunately, if you select "none" for no indent, Kindle may automatically indent the paragraph!**

- Apply the Heading 1 Style to headings. This Style should have a larger size font.
- Apply the Title Style to the title on the title "page" and to figures. The Title Style will have a larger font and will be centered.

To modify a Style (find it on the Home tab in Word 2010 or the Formatting toolbar of Word 2003), right-click it and choose Modify. Adjust the font style, size, alignment, and paragraph settings for each Style. The user can adjust the font to his or her liking on the eReader, so just use a basic, common font like Times New Roman. The user also has the option of adjusting the font size, which works best if you set Normal and FirstNormal to size 12 and make the Header 1 and Title Styles somewhat larger. Set the font color to automatic. In the paragraph options, set the linespacing to single and set First Line to 0.2" to 0.3" for Normal and 0.01" for FirstNormal (but set First Line to "none" for the Heading 1 and Title Styles). Set the justification to center for the Heading 1 and Title Styles, and to full for the Normal and FirstNormal Styles. In the paragraph options, there should be no space before or after paragraphs, except for Heading 1, which should have about 18 points set for the spacing before (because the first page of a chapter typically begins a couple of lines down from the top of the "page" – or in this case the "screen"); you might also include after space for Heading 1 to give more separation between the chapter heading and text.

You can select all and apply the Normal Style to save time from having to format paragraphs properly one at a time. However, this may remove formatting like boldface, underlining, italics, and other text features, which means you must then go through the document and restore these attributes. If you have a richly formatted document, it may be better to update the paragraphs one by one, updating each paragraph's style without disturbing formatting.

Next go through the document and apply the First-Normal Style to any non-centered paragraph that you don't want to get automatically indented (including the first paragraph of each chapter and stand-alone lines or paragraphs, such as subheadings or lines from your copyright page). Apply the Heading 1 Style to chapter headings. Apply the Title Style to the title on the title "page" and to figures.

Kindle accepts only the most basic bulleted lists, and the justification may not be perfect. Test these out carefully on all devices in the previewer before publishing. If you publish your eBook elsewhere, check their guidelines to see if they support bullets.

Pictures need to be formatted differently for eBooks than for paperbacks. For paperbacks, you want 300 DPI; this doesn't matter for eBooks. What matters for eBooks is the pixel count. 600 pixels by 800 pixels looks good on many screens, except for devices with large screens like the Kindle Fire HD, iPad, PC, or laptop. Higher pixel counts mean more memory, and memory can affect both the minimum possible price and your royalty for the Kindle eBook (and there is a maximum file size that varies by eReader; it's 50 Mb for the converted file size after uploading to Kindle, and much smaller elsewhere).

Microsoft Word may make your pictures come out smaller than the pixel count would suggest: The way to prevent this is to right-click on the picture, click Size and Position, go to the Size tab, and set the Width to 100% (the Height will adjust automatically if the Aspect Ratio is locked).

For your paperback file, you want to prevent Word from compressing images, but for your eBook file, you want to compress images to minimize the file size (they will display just fine, provided that your pixel count is sufficient and Width is set to 100%). In Word 2003, right-click on a picture, go to Format Picture > Picture, uncheck the box that says, "Apply to selected pictures only," and choose Email Resolution (96 DPI). In Word 2007 and 2010, select the image and click Compress Pictures on the Format tab at the top of the screen; also go to the File tab, select Options > Advanced, find Image Size and Quality, and uncheck the box that says, "Do not compress images in file" (you want that box checked in your paperback file, however).

All images should be inserted as JPEG files except for text and line art. Pictures that consist only of text and line art should be saved as GIF images with a maximum size of 500 pixels by 600 pixels; all other pictures should be saved as JPEG images, usually 600 pixels by 800 pixels unless you want them to appear larger on devices with large screens (then you can research the screen sizes of devices that you have in mind) and don't mind that large pixel counts add to the file size (this affects your minimum price and royalty).

If you have equations, if you can retype them as text with simple subscripts and superscripts, this is the best way to format them. However, if you have equations that require more advanced formatting (like subscripts and exponents for the same symbol or special characters, like integration symbols, that Kindle doesn't support) you can turn them into GIF images and insert them as pictures (each picture should appear on its own line with the text wrap set to in line with text). Note that it may be difficult to read detailed equations, especially on small screens like an iPhone. Test out equations with the previewer on all devices to see if they are acceptable before publishing.

Many of the special symbols that you can create in Microsoft Word don't show up in eReaders – instead, they will display as question marks (?) or a jumble of strange characters. Therefore, you want to make sure that you don't use any unsupported symbols. The following Kindle page lists supported characters for the Kindle devices:

https://images-na.ssl-images-amazon.com
/images/G/01/digital/otp/help/Latin1.gif

There may be a few common characters that Kindle supports, which don't appear on the graphic given in the previous link. For example, hold down Alt and type:

- 0150 for an en dash (–)
- 0151 for an em dash (—)
- 0147 for an open curly quote (")
- 0148 for a closed curly quote (")
- 0145 for an open single quote (')
- 0146 for a closed single quote or curly apostrophe (')

You should check each device carefully in the preview to be sure that the characters come out okay. Supported characters may not format correctly on all devices when you make them with Word's AutoCorrect feature (e.g. typing space hyphen space to generate an en dash through AutoCorrect) instead of using the Alt codes.

One problem with eBook formatting is that you can't predict where a line will break (since the eBook can be read on anything from the size of an iPhone to a PC, and the user can adjust the font size and style). Kindle gives you a little control with the non-breaking space. Hold down Ctrl then Shift and press the spacebar to create a non-breaking space (press the Show/Hide button on the paragraph group of the Home tab if you want to see the difference visually). Use a non-breaking space when you have two symbols that naturally go together, like 3 hrs or 8 kg. In the case of 3 hrs, if the "hrs" extends onto the next line, this forces the 3 to go with it. Avoid using non-breaking spaces with long words or where it's non-essential, otherwise it can create large gaps in justified text (especially on devices with small screens).

Similarly, you can't predict where blank line spaces may appear: A blank linespace can appear at the top or bottom of the screen, for example, where it may not be noticed. For this reason, it's not a good idea to use two consecutive blank linespaces to create a section break in an eBook. It's better to use three asterisks (* * *) between blank linespaces. That way, the section break will be visible regardless of where it appears vertically on the device's screen. An alternative to the asterisks is a glyph or design that matches the theme of the book without distracting the reader.

Using Shift + Enter can yield a more predictable blank linespace in an eBook. Don't use Shift + Enter at the end of a paragraph in your paperback, as it will make the line fill the margin. If you do this in your eBook file, the last line of the paragraph won't look good on your monitor, but when you view it on the preview, it will probably look fine (as always, test out how it looks on each device in the preview). If you want to create a blank linespace in your eBook, use Shift + Enter twice (once at the end of the previous paragraph, then again for the blank line). For example, if you want to insert blank lines between elements of your table of contents (or anywhere else), use the Shift + Enter method for more predictable results. Use this to create blank lines before and after images, too. Don't worry that the last line of the previous paragraph will look funny on your monitor in Word (as long as it looks fine in the preview).

A table of contents must be formatted much differently for an eBook than for a print book. Instead of including page numbers, use bookmark hyperlinks. This lets the reader click on the bookmark and go directly to that chapter or section of the eBook.

First, you must create the bookmarks before you can insert bookmark hyperlinks into the table of contents. Find the first item that will appear in your table of contents (e.g. the Introduction or Chapter 1). Go to the actual heading in the book (not the heading from your table of contents). Don't bookmark the heading itself. Instead, insert a blank line above the heading, press the spacebar a few times at the beginning of the blank line, highlight these spaces, and apply the FirstNormal Style to the spaces (which appear above the heading).

Highlight the spaces on the blank line above the heading then Insert > Bookmark. Type the name of the section without spaces (like Chapter1, not Chapter 1) and click Add. Repeat all of these steps for every component of the table of contents (but bookmark the actual headings in the book; don't bookmark headings from the table of contents).

Once you've made the bookmarks, you're ready to add bookmark hyperlinks to your table of contents. Now highlight the first item on your table of contents list (e.g. the Introduction or Chapter 1 – you should have a space in the text in your list and in your headings, just don't name the bookmarks with spaces), go to Insert > Hyperlink, select Place in This Document, choose the corresponding bookmark, and press OK. Repeat these steps for each item of your table of contents (but don't link the table of contents heading to itself). Don't use any bookmarks that Word may have generated automatically; make sure that any bookmark you add is one that you made yourself.

Bookmarks have other uses besides just making a table of contents. For example, suppose you refer to Appendix A. If you turn this text into a bookmark, the reader can jump directly to the appendix by activating the hyperlink. These are called internal hyperlinks. You make these bookmarks the same way that you make the active table of contents.

You can also add external hyperlinks. For example, if you provide a link to a website in your book (you should have your own author website or blog, which you can make for free, and include it with an about the author page in the back of your book; you can also link to your social media pages this way), this is an external hyperlink. To create an external hyperlink, if Word automatically converted your url to an active hyperlink, deactivate it (right-click it to get this option), then highlight the url (once deactivated), go to Insert > Hyperlink, type the full web address (including the http:// part, otherwise it won't work in the eReader).

Check all of your hyperlinks to ensure that they work properly. Click on the table of contents hyperlinks and internal bookmarks to see if they take you to the proper destination. Press Ctrl and left-click the external hyperlinks to open a browser and check that each url works correctly.

Editing/Formatting Resources

- You can find free editing and formatting articles on my blog: www.chrismcmullen.wordpress.com. Once there, click the Editing/Formatting tab.
- CreateSpace has articles on formatting: Click the Free Publishing Resources tab at the top of the website to access these.
- Although you can self-publish for free, if you need help, CreateSpace does offer paid editing and formatting services. From the homepage, click the Books tab, then choose Editing or Layout and Design to learn more. Ask if you'll get to

keep the edited file (and in what format), and what happens if you need to make changes after the process is complete.

- Many small publishers who actively participate in the CreateSpace community forum offer their editing and formatting services. As with shopping for any service, try to learn about the person's character and qualifications, and seek objective opinions from someone who has used the service. Ask to have a sample chapter edited or formatted as a token of what to expect. Read your contract carefully. Find out exactly what you're getting for your investment.

- Amazon has a free guide for basic Kindle formatting called *Building Your Book for Kindle*. You can read it on a PC or Mac.

- If you need help with formatting issues, for paperback help, try searching the CreateSpace community help forum and posting your question if you don't find the answer there, and for Kindle help, try using the Kindle community help forum. Chances are that someone else has had the exact same problem and will be happy to share the solution.

- The Kindle help pages (see the link below) have many useful tips.

https://kdp.amazon.com
/help?topicId=A3R2IZDC42DJW6

- It is possible to pay someone to format your Kindle eBook for you. CreateSpace offers this service. While you shouldn't accept the free offer to send your PDF to Kindle (because PDF's tend to format poorly as eBooks), their paid services will result in an actual eBook format, not a PDF. Alternatively, Kindle lists a variety of companies who specialize in Kindle conversion services (see the link below):

https://kdp.amazon.com
/help?topicId=A3RRQXI478DDG7

6 Designing the Book Cover

DESIGNING A GOOD book cover is important because it's the first thing the reader sees. We would like readers to judge our books by the content, but a shopper has to first decide whether or not to even read the content. Potential buyers can read reviews, the description of your book, see the cover, and look inside your book on its webpage at Amazon.com. Since the cover is one of the first things a shopper might look at, you want the front cover to make a good impression, the back cover to include information that describes your book well and helps to sell your book, and the cover to appear professional.

A cover functions as an important marketing tool:

- When customers see your book, based on the cover they will decide in average of three seconds whether or not to click on it and learn more.
- Many customers browse for books by viewing several thumbnails on a page of search results. More appealing covers attract more customers.
- Customers are much more likely to click on your book to learn more about it if your book's cover attracts your specific target audience.
- A book cover helps an author brand the image of a book. If a customer recognizes your cover from having seen it in the past, this improves your chances of catching the customer's interest.
- A poor cover suggests little effort was put into the content; an appealing cover seems professional.

You have five options for getting a book cover:

- Hire a cover designer. It's reasonable to spend $100 to $300 for a custom design.
- Shop for premade covers. Many sell for $10 to $100. It's hard to get a perfect match for your book, and there may be other covers like yours.
- Design your own cover for free. You can draw your own images on the computer, take photographs, scan images (hand-drawn usually doesn't work well on a cover), or shop for free stock images (make sure they are 300 DPI).
- Make your own cover, but invest a small amount of money in stock images (be sure they are 300 DPI) that fit your cover well.
- Use Cover Creator, CreateSpace's free tool. Your design will be limited in some ways and your book may look like many other covers created by this tool, but it's convenient and easy.

I've designed almost all of my covers myself. In 2013, I invested in some covers, paying $300 each, and am very pleased with the results. Investing $100 to $300 in a book cover is a lot of money to spend: If your royalty is a few dollars, you may have to sell a hundred books just to break even. If you wind up selling just a couple of books per week, it may take several months to recover your expense.

However, if you have a highly marketable book, a professional-looking cover that attracts your specific target audience can make the difference between selling several copies per day versus just one or two per day. The challenge is predicting how marketable your book is and what effect the cover will have.

Did you do the research prescribed in Chapter 3? This data can help you see how well similar books are doing. Your book may or may not do as well, but at least this gives you something to judge by. Other things to consider include: How confident are you in your book? Have you published previous books to help you judge your potential? How motivated are you to market your book? Are you prepared for the possibility of the investment not paying off?

If you choose to hire a cover designer, do some research first. At a minimum, you want reasons to expect a much better cover than you could make yourself (a portfolio of previous covers may help you judge this – also see if there are any in your genre). You want a cover that will look professional and attract your specific target audience (so browsing similar covers will help you see what those readers are accustomed to).

You could make a cover yourself or pay for a low-cost cover to start with, reserving the option to upgrade to a better cover later. Some authors do this hoping to learn if the book is worth it first, or to acquire the funds to pay for a cover from the initial royalties. The main disadvantage of this is that the first three months are your best opportunity to attract sales, since your book will be visible in the Last 30 Days and Last 90 Days new release categories when it's first published.

In this chapter, I will show you how you can make your cover – in whole or in part – by yourself using Microsoft Word. If you have access to PhotoShop and some experience with PhotoShop, you have the potential to create a better cover there (but there are also some pitfalls of using PhotoShop, such as filters that sometimes do more harm than good). If you do make your own cover, it will help to keep your initial investment to a minimum. This way, you won't put yourself in a position where you need to sell a hundred or more copies of your book just to break even. If you can write your own book, you can surely design and make your own cover – and a good one – following the prescription described in this chapter. At the very least, try it yourself and see how it turns out; that way, if you do hire help, you will see firsthand how much that improves on your own effort.

You can make a professional cover using Microsoft Word. If you have Microsoft Word 2007, you might obtain better results saving your file as a .doc file (the 2003 format), unless you use features specific to Word 2007, in which case you must use .docx to retain those features. I encountered a few bugs designing covers with 2007; I haven't had these problems with 2003 or 2010. The .docx format works better for me with Word 2010.

After discussing the cover design in the next section, I will describe specifically how to make your cover in Microsoft Word. If you create your cover using different software, the design of your cover may follow a similar prescription and many of the design tips may still apply – so you may wish to read the following section even if not using Word. In the last section of this chapter, I explain how to use Microsoft Word's drawing tools.

Designing a Professional Cover

Study the covers that you see on a variety of books, including books that are or are not similar to yours. This will give you ideas for what features to include on your cover and help inspire your own cover style.

Obviously, you need to include the title, which should stand out well in large letters, the subtitle, and the author's name. The title and subtitle should attract the reader's attention and, especially if your work is nonfiction, give the reader an idea of what your book is about. If any words are emphasized (e.g. with a larger font size), they should be key words.

Some nicely drawn (usually, not by hand) artwork or a photograph on the front cover can help catch attention and lend your book a professional appearance. You would like readers to imagine your book sitting in their hands. The cover should be attractive. What is attractive to one may not be attractive to another, but you want the cover to be appealing to most of your audience.

Most back covers include text that will help to sell the book to a potential customer. On Amazon, the back cover will be visible where the Look Inside feature is accessed, but the back cover is more valuable for people who see your book in person (such as on a customer's coffee table). Most online buyers see just the thumbnail image of your front cover until they buy your book and it arrives in the mail, so it's very important for your front cover to form a good impression.

CreateSpace will make the ISBN and UPC bar code for you. They will identify the exact location and size (within their printing tolerance) of this label so you can design your cover around it. With the instructions that follow, you will be able to predict the UPC's location.

Your book will be more professional if you include the title and author's name on the spine. However, CreateSpace only permits text to be included on the spine if the book has at least 102 pages. The spine text must also be narrow enough to leave 0.0625" between the text and the spine edges. For narrow spines, writing the spine text in CAPS will allow you to use the largest possible font size (since some lowercase letters, like g and q, have tails that limit the usable space).

It's important that the spine label be centered very well on your cover file so that it prints as professionally as possible – it will stand out like a sore thumb if it is off-center. You do have to allow for a small printing tolerance, though (an estimate may be available on the publisher's webpage). Eventually, you will receive a proof of your book, but it is just one sample; if afterward you order multiple copies of your book, you will obtain a better measure of how reliable the printing is. (Overall, in my experience viewing over a thousand copies in person, it is very good, but nothing is perfect so you want to understand any limitations.)

If you plan to try to market your book to any bookstores, you will need a label on the spine to help customers identify your book when it is sitting on a bookshelf. Some bookstores will simply not purchase books that do not have a spine label.

Including a cover price is optional. Some retailers in the Expanded Distribution channel may wish to mark up the price of your book, so having a cover price might frustrate customers who pay more than that. If you succeed in getting local bookstores to stock your book, chances are that they will place a label on your book anyway, so including a cover price won't matter to them (but if they wish to charge more for your book, again any cover price might pose a problem). You can see that I tend to include prices on my covers. I did this because many readers are accustomed to seeing this; the more your book looks like what your audience is used to, the better it will fit the buyer's eye. However, many indie authors prefer to leave the price off the cover, especially if they intend to sell copies to local bookstores.

> Your cover should include – at a minimum – a title, subtitle, author's name, ISBN with UPC barcode (automatic), spine label (if the width permits), back cover text (optional, but can be helpful), and front cover art.

Even if your book interior is black-and-white, your cover will print in color. So take advantage of this and use color when you create your cover.

However, color images often do not print exactly the same way as they appear on the screen. This is not the fault of the publisher, but a problem that plagues the publishing industry in general. The publisher's printing process is excellent, but for technical reasons relating to the color scheme used to print an image on the screen versus the color scheme used to print an image on paper, your book cover (and interior if it is color, too) may have slight variations in color compared to what you expect from viewing your cover on the screen.

Computer monitors use a RGB (red, green, blue) color addition scheme. Any color can be created by combining the right amounts of red, green, and blue at any point on the screen. Printers, on the other hand, use a CMYK (cyan, magenta, yellow, black) color subtraction scheme. The technical reasons for the differences have to do with the physical processes involved – i.e. the difference between producing an image on a screen that emits light of a given color versus combining pigments on paper that reflect light of given color. (This is actually an engineering issue – it's not like selling hot dogs in packages of six and hot dog buns in packages of eight.)

Here's what this means to you: Using the RGB color scheme, monitors can make virtually any color, but printers are much more limited with their use of the CMYK subtraction scheme. Thus, the printer may not be able to reproduce every color you can view on your monitor exactly the way it appears on your screen. The printer the publisher uses is not the same as your own home printer, so a color could print one way in your house but slightly differently in your book.

One common problem is that images tend to look much brighter when displayed on a monitor and much darker in print. Most authors strive to perfect the image as seen on the monitor, only to be frustrated to see it appear much darker on the printed cover. Here is a tip: Print out a sample with a deskjet printer to give you a rough idea of how much darker it might appear in print;

order a proof of your book with the tentative cover for a better indication. You really want your cover to look great both in print and on the monitor, since many customers will first see it when shopping online and later hold your book in their hands.

When you draw your own artwork and make your text, you may minimize problems if you stick to standard RGB colors. When selecting the color of an object in Format, choose More Colors > Custom and enter the RGB values. You can find the RGB values for many standard colors in the table below. Note that in Word 2007 and later, many of the preset colors (like green) are not standard colors.

Color	Red	Green	Blue
aqua	0	255	255
black	0	0	0
blue	0	0	255
fuchsia	255	0	255
gray	128	128	128
green	0	128	0
lime	0	255	0
maroon	128	0	0
navy	0	0	128
olive	128	128	0
purple	128	0	128
red	255	0	0
silver	192	192	192
teal	0	128	128
white	255	255	255
yellow	255	255	0

Fortunately, when your PDF files are ready, you first purchase an inexpensive proof copy, so you will see exactly how the colors print. If you are not happy with your proof, you have as much time as you like to make revisions. Once you do approve a proof, you should know approximately what your customers are receiving: Their copies will look just like your proof, within reasonable printing tolerances.

If you publish with CreateSpace, you can use the Cover Creator feature. However, it is pretty straightforward to follow the prescription outlined in the next section to make your own professional cover. Doing it yourself gives you the flexibility to design a cover exactly the way you want it. With Cover Creator, your cover may look like many other books.

Drawing Your Cover in Microsoft Word

Microsoft Word has a tendency to make images at a lower resolution, since it's generally intended for showing images on a screen (where 96 DPI is just fine) or printing on a household printer. This helps to reduce the active memory. These tendencies are a problem when publishing a book, however. Images print best when they are 300 DPI or greater.

Before inserting or drawing any images, you want to disable Word's automatic tendencies. You can find instructions for how to do this in the next section (following the pages of sample covers).

> Disable Word's automatic compression feature before inserting or drawing any images. Skip to the next section to learn how to do this.

You need to have your book cover saved in one file and your book interior saved in a separate file. So open a blank document in which to begin designing your book cover. Go to Page Setup in the File tab of Word 2003 or Page Layout in Word 2007 and up to set the page size. Set the page size exactly to the size of the full-spread cover including bleeds. If you submit a PDF cover larger than this, it increases the chances of encountering readjustments during file review.

Determine your cover's full-spread (i.e. with front, spine, and back together) size as follows:

- width = trim width x 2 + spine width + 0.25"
- height = trim height + 0.25"
- spine width = 0.002252" x page count for black-and-white interior on white pages
- spine width = 0.0025" x page count for black-and-white interior on cream pages
- spine width = 0.002347" x page count for color interior on white pages

Here, trim width and trim height form the trim size of your book. For example, if you choose a trim size of 6" x 9", the trim width is 6" and the trim height is 9". If your book has 130 pages with a black-and-white interior on white paper, then your cover width will be 6" x 2" + 0.002252" x 130 + 0.25" = 12.54" and your cover height will be 9" + 0.25" = 9.25". In this example, you would set the page width to 12.54" and the page height to 9.25" in Microsoft Word.

It will be handy to zoom in and out periodically in the View tab. Sometimes you'll want to see how the cover looks as a whole page, other times you'll want to zoom to see just the front or back cover, and when perfecting the details you'll want to zoom in further for a closer look. Note that the alignment may be a little off when viewing the entire cover as a whole page, whereas 100% is usually more reliable (also, zooming in far in Word 2003 has some alignment issues). Print out a test copy and you won't have to wonder.

If you are not already familiar with drawing objects in Microsoft Word, you might want to read the tutorial in the following section to become better acquainted with the drawing tools and then return to this section.

Insert a rectangle. Right-click on the rectangle and change the size to the trim size of your book (e.g. 6" x 9"). Change the fill color to no fill. After removing the fill color, you will need to click on the border of the rectangle in order to grab it. Copy and paste this rectangle so that you have two identical large rectangles. Make a third rectangle (with no fill) with a width equal to your spine width (this is defined in the previous bullet list, you can find a calculator for this on CreateSpace's website, and will also find this value after you submit your interior file) and the height equal to the height of your trim size (e.g. 0.29" x 9").

Position them roughly so that the spine width rectangle is in the center and the other two large rectangles are just to its left and right. Grab all three of these rectangles and align their tops with the Align tool from the Format tab. Then grab the left rectangle and use the left/right arrow keys to move it horizontally until its right edge matches up with the spine width rectangle's left edge. Also join the right rectangle's left edge to the spine width rectangle's right edge.

Group the three rectangles together into a single image. Then unclick the object, right-click on it, and go to Format Object > Layout > Advanced, where you can choose to center it horizontally and vertically on the page. Now your cover will be centered on your file. At some point in your work you may want to ungroup these rectangles (at least temporarily) – e.g. if you want to center a picture or WordArt with just one of the three rectangles by using the align command.

Make a new rectangle (it's okay to leave a white fill for this one) and change its size to 0.25" x 0.25". Copy and paste it until you have 8 of these squares. Put these 8 squares in the corners of the front and back cover rectangles (the large rectangle on the right corresponds to the front cover, while the large rectangle on the left corresponds to the back cover). The purpose of these 8 squares is to define the active area of the front and back covers. Don't put any text within 0.25" of the border defined by these squares.

Make a new rectangle (white fill is okay) that is 2" wide and 1.2" high. Put it in the bottom right of your back cover rectangle such that its lower-right corner matches the upper-left corner of the 0.25" x 0.25" square that you just put there. This is where your ISBN and UPC bar code will print. Anything you put in this space, such as artwork, will be covered up by the bar code. So don't put any text (or anything else you don't want to get covered up) in this area.

Select all of these objects – the original three rectangles for the front and back cover and spine, the 8 squares, and the bar code rectangle – and group them together. These are your guides. You will want to delete the guides when you are completely finished so that the guides don't print on your actual cover. If you ungroup these rectangles at some point during your work (useful, for example, for aligning objects with just one of these rectangles), you can regroup them afterward.

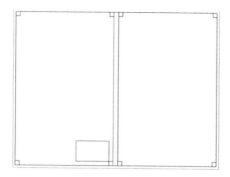

Thus far, your document should look like the previous image (where the back cover is on the left, the front cover is on the right, and the ISBN/bar code rectangle appears near the bottom right of the back cover).

The background color or pattern for your cover needs to extend beyond the cover size (i.e. all the way to the outer rectangle). Your cover prints on a larger size sheet from which your cover is cut out. So you need your background to extend beyond the size of your cover to allow for tolerance in the printing and cutting processes. This is why the actual page size extends 0.125" beyond the front and back cover edges. Your background image should completely fill the outer rectangle.

The background image could simply be a rectangle the same size as the page and properly centered with a simple fill color or gradient, or it could be a picture (ideally at least 300 DPI). Click on your background image and change its Order to the back (or place it behind text in Page Layout) so that all other images and text appear in front of your background. I recommend inserting this background rectangle after the remainder of your cover is complete – it will be easier to select, move, and alter other objects in your cover if the background image is not there. However, you might want to have the background color in mind to make sure that your color scheme works well.

Any art or images must either extend all the way to the edge of the outer rectangle (i.e. beyond the 3 cover rectangles), or must not get closer to the cover edges than 0.25" (the 8 squares help to mark this area). Text must also not get closer to the cover edges than 0.25".

Add separate textboxes (or WordArt) for your title, subtitle, author name, and other text that you might include. Change the outline to no color to remove the rectangle from the textbox. Change the fill color to no color also in order to prevent its fill color from blocking out other images. If you insert WordArt, remove any shadow that may appear in the default. Choose a large font size for your title. You might want to divide your title up into two or more textboxes if you want a couple of the words to appear much different than the others. Make sure that your title stands out well and is very readable in terms of size and color. Center the title, subtitle, and author's name relative to one another and to the front cover rectangle.

Insert WordArt to make the spine label. Choose a horizontal line for the WordArt shape. You will probably want a fill color, but may not want an outline color, for this text (but neither for the shape – i.e. compare the similar tools Shape Fill and Text Fill). Type the title, then several spaces, then the author's name. Some trial and error will help you get the spacing right. You can adjust both the size of the WordArt as well as the font style and size in order to change the appearance of the spine label (but be careful to preserve the aspect ratio).

Right-click the spine label to change the Layout to in front of text. Now you can click on the spine label to rotate it 90° to the right (not left). Center it in the spine rectangle. Leave a little room around the spine text for printing tolerance, making the spine text smaller if necessary. Check that the orientation of your spine matches that of books that you have. (If you have a book with a few hundred pages or more, your spine might be wide enough to include a spine label that is not rotated. However, most books have a rotated spine label.)

Spine text must be at least 0.0625" from the spine edges (otherwise, CreateSpace will resize your spine text). If your spine is narrow (not much longer than 102 pages), write your spine text in CAPS to maximize the available space (since some lowercase letters like g and q have tails). If your page count is 100 pages or less, you can't include spine text.

Add some textboxes for your back cover (with no shape fill or shape outline). Draw interest to your book. What is your book about? How is it distinguished from the competition (but don't put your competition down)? Do you have qualifications worth mentioning? If you have any book reviews yet, you can use quotes from these (citing your source if it is a magazine or website, and ensuring that you have permission to use the review quote). Read several book covers to get ideas for what kind of information you might want to include on your back cover.

Textboxes and WordArt have changed somewhat from 2003 thru 2010. In Word 2010, it's easy to change the font size (working in .docx mode). In some of the older versions of Word, it may seem intuitive to resize WordArt, for example, but in such a way so as to change the aspect ratio of the text. If possible, change the font size to resize your cover text. If you must resize the box itself, first lock the aspect ratio (right-click and choose Size and Position).

For artwork, you can draw your own artwork (using the Microsoft Word drawing tools described in the next section or a different drawing program) or you can insert photographs – or both. If you are working with photos, you might prefer to open them in a program designed for viewing and editing photos, then crop them and format them, if needed, before inserting them into your document (cropping and editing images in the native program – rather than adjusting them in Word – and inserting them as you want them to appear may help to maximize their resolution in the Word file, along with other precautions described in the next section).

> Don't forget to remove the cover guide before you upload your book cover for publishing.

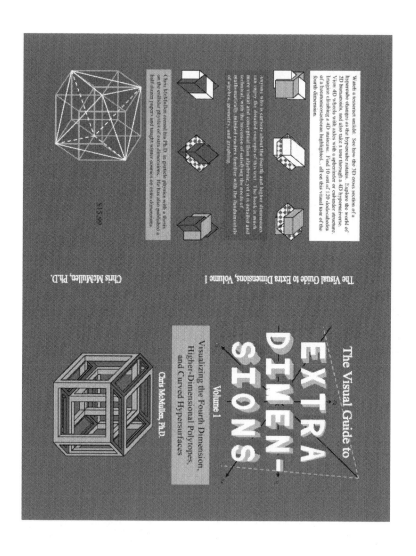

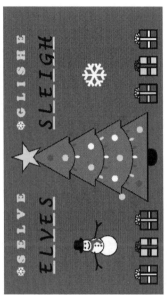

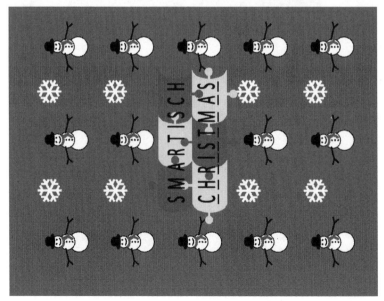

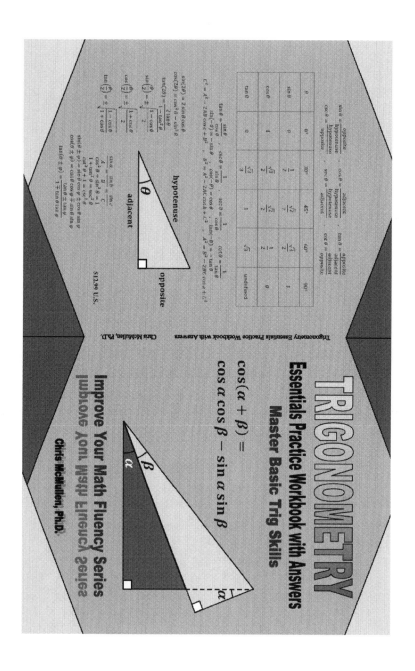

GOLF WORD SCRAMBLES   Chris McMullen and Carolyn Kivett

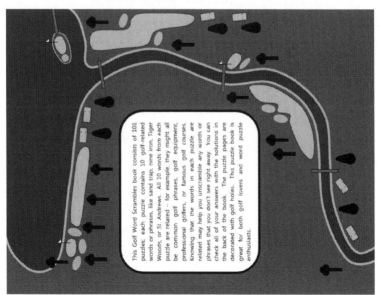

This Golf Word Scrambles book consists of 101 puzzles; each puzzle contains 10 golf-related words or phrases, like sand trap, nine iron, Tiger Woods, or St. Andrews. All 10 words from each puzzle are related – for example, they might all be common golf phrases, golf equipment, professional golfers, or famous golf courses. Knowing that the words in each puzzle are related may help you unscramble any words or phrases that you don't see right away. You can check all of your answers with the solutions in the back of the book. The puzzle pages are decorated with golf holes. This puzzle book is great for both golf lovers and word puzzle enthusiasts.

This book will show you how to prepare and submit files to a print-on-demand self-publishing service that is part of the Amazon group of companies – a self-publishing service that you can trust, which requires virtually no investment (just a few dollars for the cost of your book plus shipping). Following the steps outlined in this guide, your book can be selling in as little as a week once your manuscript is completed.

The author, Chris McMullen, has self-published over a dozen different types of books on Amazon.com. He is experienced with the techniques and details, and is sharing his knowledge with you through this guide. This handy reference takes you through all of the steps of the self-publishing process, from writing your manuscript to editing and formatting to preparing PDF files to publishing your book to low-cost promotional strategies for improving sales.

$11.99 USA

MCMULLEN

HOW TO SELF-PUBLISH A BOOK ON AMAZON.COM

HOW TO SELF-PUBLISH a Book on AMAZON.COM

Chris McMullen

UPDATED 2014 EXPANDED

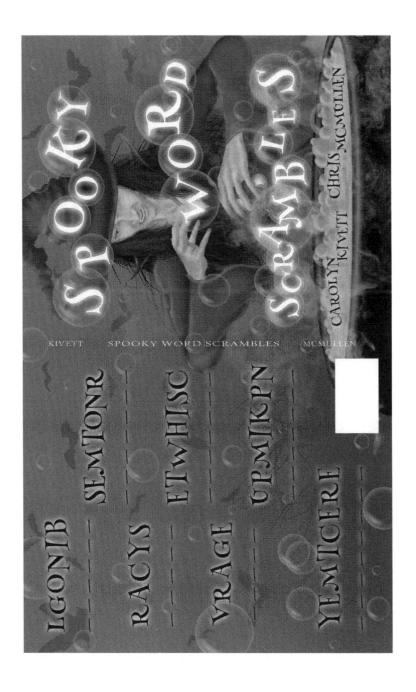

Below are some sample eBook covers:

Using the Microsoft Word Drawing Tools

Before drawing or inserting any pictures into the Word file for either your interior or cover, you must first disable Word's tendency to automatically compress your images. Even that won't prevent Word from reducing the resolution of your pictures: There are a couple of other things you need to know, too.

Here is how you can turn off automatic picture compression in Word (you must do this again for every Word file that you create, and do it before inserting or drawing any images):

- In Word 2003, right-click on a picture (ideally, do this the first time you insert a picture; if you don't have any images in your file yet, you can insert one temporarily), select the Show Picture Toolbar, click Compress Pictures, select All Pictures in Document, and uncheck the box next to Compress Pictures.
- In Word 2007, right-click on a picture, go to the Format tab, click Compress Images, uncheck the box marked "Apply to selected pictures only," select Options, and uncheck the box marked "Automatically perform basic compression on save."
- In Word 2010, click the File tab, scroll down to the bottom of the list (it might be hidden at first, in which case you just need to scroll below Help

to find it), select Advanced, scroll down to find Image Size and Quality, and check the box marked "Do not compress images in file."

Ideally, you want images to have 300 DPI for your print book, but Word likes to reduce them to as little as 96 DPI. For your eBook file, you want 96 DPI instead, as that will save memory. Create separate files for your paperback and eBook, but remember to make any revisions to the text to both files. For your eBook, you want to do the opposite of the instructions above, compressing images automatically instead of turning picture compression off (for your eBook, you want 96 DPI).

You must take additional steps to avoid picture compression for your paperback. In addition to turning off picture compression, don't crop or resize any pictures after inserting them into Word (otherwise, Word may reduce the resolution). If you've already cropped or resized pictures that you inserted into Word from files, delete those and reinsert them (you *can* crop or resize them in the native program). Also, don't copy/paste images into Word: You must go to the Insert tab to add pictures if you want to avoid having the resolution reduced. In the next chapter, we'll learn that you must also print to PDF via a Word-to-PDF converter instead of using the convenient Save As feature (since Save As PDF results in lower DPI for your images).

For your print book, deactivate Word's automatic picture compression before drawing or inserting any pictures. Don't crop or resize images after inserting them from files. Use Insert > Picture instead of copy/paste. To create the PDF file, don't use Word's convenient Save As PDF feature if you have images in your file. These actions will reduce the DPI of your images.

> For your eBook, you instead want to activate automatic picture compression. You want 96 DPI for your eBook, but 300 DPI for your print book.

If you use Microsoft Word 2003, I highly recommend that you click the Tools tab, choose Options, select the General tab, and uncheck the box that says, "Automatically create drawing canvas when inserting Auto-Shapes." I find it much more convenient and flexible to put shapes anywhere I want on the page rather than the confines of the drawing canvas. (In Word 2007 and beyond, there is no default canvas to worry about.)

In Microsoft Word 2007, the various drawing tools can be found in tabs at the top of the page. You begin with the Insert tab, selecting one of the options in Illustrations, such as Shapes. Once you have a diagram going, you may need to go to the Home tab and choose to select (or deselect) objects by checking (or unchecking) this box – you can find this at the far right of the Home tab, with the Editing options. If you have a drawing object selected, a new tab will appear – Format. Yet other drawing tools are located at the far right of the Page Layout tab, with the Arrange options.

Here is where to find the Microsoft Word 2007 and 2010 drawing tools:

• Insert tab: This where you can insert shapes, text-boxes, and WordArt. Start your diagram here.

• Format tab: This has most of the drawing tools and options. This tab is only accessible when you have selected an object that has already been drawn. From here, you can change the fill and outline colors and styles, picture layout, and much more.

• Page Layout tab: This tab has Arrange options. It is useful for grouping objects together, aligning objects, rotating objects, and positioning objects in front of text, behind text, or in line with text. You can find these same options in the Format tab, too.

• Home tab: If you want to select multiple objects, you can go to Select and check a box to do this (then to select text you have to go back and uncheck this box). In Word 2007, you can then draw an outline rectangle by dragging the mouse and any drawing objects inside this rectangle will all be selected. There is also a handy Selection Pane on the Format toolbar in Word 2010.

In Microsoft Word 2003, all of the drawing tools are conveniently located in the same place – a drawing toolbar. Simply click the View tab, click Toolbars, and check the Drawing toolbar.

In any version of Microsoft Word, you can access many of the drawing options by right-clicking on an object – e.g. under Format Autoshape or Format Object.

> Many of the drawing features can be found by right-clicking on an image.

You need to understand the grid to help align objects well (the align tools on the Format tab can help, too). Alignment tends to be more reliable when the View is set to 100% (or to the page width, except for large page widths, like 12").

Explore and understand the grid before you begin drawing. Students (and others) tell me that they have tried drawing in Microsoft Word 2003 and found it to be very limited. In every case, this turned out to be because they didn't understand the grid options. Once you understand the grid options well, you will be able to use it to your benefit – instead of it preventing you from what you would like to accomplish (Microsoft Word

2007 is slightly more restrictive than Microsoft Word 2003, but I expect that this came about as an effort to reduce file problems associated with active memory required to work with your document).

Experiment with turning the grid on or off. In Microsoft Word 2003, you can separately choose whether or not to snap objects to the grid. In Word 2007 and 2010, find Grid Settings by clicking Align from the Format tab or the Page Layout tab.

You must be flexible with the grid options (i.e. don't insist on always having the grid turned on or off). There will be times when you need the grid on and others when you need it off, and in Microsoft Word 2003 there will be times when you do want to snap objects to the grid and times when you don't. Keep the grid options on your mind: If you're having trouble aligning things the way you would like, you probably need to change the grid options.

You will want the grid on (and to snap objects to the grid) if you are trying to join two objects at a specific point, when these points on each object both lie at grid corners. The grid is also useful for making horizontal or vertical lines, or for making one object a given multiple of times wider or taller than another object (you can also set the width and height precisely in Format > Size).

You will want to turn the grid off (and not snap objects to the grid) if you are trying to attach an object to a precise point that lies between gridlines. This is also sometimes visually useful.

Sometimes you need the grid off, sometimes on. It pays to be flexible with the grid (and snapping) options.

Suppose you want to join two objects together and have them connect at a precise point. For simplicity, imagine that you have one vertical and one horizontal line segment, which you would like to join at the endpoints. If your grid is off and you are not snapping objects to the grid, if you try to line these up with your eyeball, they will not match up perfectly – this will look less professional when you print the diagram. (Zooming in considerably does not prevent this problem.) If instead you turn the grid on and snap objects to the grid (remember, you have to choose these separately in Microsoft Word 2003), it is much easier to line these up precisely. The Align tool in the Format tab can also help to align images precisely (but look closely; in Word 2010, for example, you can sometimes get funny results if any of the images have been rotated, for example; sometimes, you get better results manually).

In the illustration that follows, the diagram on the left was made without snapping the objects to the grid whereas the diagram on the right was made by snapping the objects to the grid. Look closely at the corner and you will see the distinction. If you want to create professional diagrams, this is an important distinction. (This particular image can alternatively be drawn with the freeform tool.)

On the other hand, sometimes you want to position something precisely, but if the grid is on and you are snapping objects to the grid, you will be prevented from putting the object exactly where you want it. In this case, you need to choose not snap objects to the grid (turn the grid off in Microsoft Word 2007 or 2010).

If you are snapping objects to the grid, it will be easier to draw very horizontal and vertical lines. If you are not, you can still draw very horizontal and vertical lines if you draw them with care: Look closely and you will see that the line appears smoother on the screen when it is horizontal or vertical, and a little less smooth when it is slightly off.

If you need to grab two or more drawing objects, you can drag your mouse to draw a rectangle around the objects, in which case any object inside the rectangle will be selected. Note that I don't mean to insert a rectangle shape. In Microsoft Word 2007, go to Select on the far right of the Home tab and check the box for selecting drawing objects (in Microsoft Word 2003, just click the arrow on the drawing toolbar), then you can select objects by making this rectangle. In Word 2010, you can't select with such a rectangle, but you can turn on the Selection Pane.

Alternatively, you can grab one object, press Ctrl, and continue holding Ctrl as you grab the other objects.

It just takes a little exploratory practice to master the drawing tools. Once you get used to them they turn out to be pretty intuitive.

So let's get started. Open a blank document in Microsoft Word and prepare yourself to get acquainted with some of the drawing tools and features. We'll discuss how to insert various shapes and make diagrams from them and you will develop Microsoft Word drawing skills by trying this on your computer as you read this book. Don't be shy: You will learn much better by trying; simply reading will probably not be very helpful.

Grab the line tool from the Insert tab (or drawing toolbar in Microsoft Word 2003). Position the cursor at a point where you would like to start drawing the line segment, then press and hold the mouse button down to drag the line out as far as you like and in the direction you want, and release the mouse button when your line segment is ready.

Try to make a horizontal or vertical line both with and without snapping objects to the grid. Notice how the line is smoothest when it is horizontal or vertical, but a little less so when it is slightly off.

Make two different line segments and explore your manual alignment options both with and without snapping objects to the grid, as we discussed in a previous example. Also, explore the Align tools available on the Format tab.

Now try to insert an arrow instead of a line. Try reversing the arrow's direction or making a double arrow. Change the size and style of the arrow.

Insert other AutoShapes, such as circles and rectangles. Choose different fill and line colors. Change the line thickness and style. Explore some of the fill effects, like the gradient.

See if you can rotate and flip an AutoShape. You can rotate an object 90 degrees with standard buttons. In Microsoft Word 2003, you can also choose Free Rotate. In any version, you can right-click the object and choose any degree value from 0 to 360 degrees for its orientation: Format AutoShape (or Object), go to the Size tab, and enter the rotation angle. Try entering a few different rotation angles to explore this option.

Select a rectangle and adjust its size using the mouse. Stretch it out horizontally, then vertically, then diagonally. Now right-click to format the object, and in the Size tab check the box to lock the aspect ratio. This does not guarantee that the aspect ratio will not change. You can still stretch it horizontally or vertically. If you want to preserve the aspect ratio, check this box and then stretch it only along a diagonal. Go back to the Size tab and note that you can manually enter the dimensions of the object instead of stretching it out visually.

With multiple drawing objects on your screen, try selecting two or more of them and aligning them in various ways – center, middle, or top, for example. Group them together. Select the group and then click on one of the objects: Notice how this results in an extra set of markers to indicate the boundaries of the selected AutoShape in addition to the entire object. Try this again if necessary to see the difference between selecting the grouped object and selecting an object within the group. It's important to understand the distinction so that you can manipulate grouped objects correctly. If you have the group selected, instead of one object in the group, you can format the group as a whole. Try rotating the group.

Change the layout of the group by right-clicking the group, choosing Format Object, and going to the Layout tab. See what happens when you choose in line with text. Write some text. Grab the object and move it to a different position in the text to understand this formatting option. Try to center it on its own line (use the Enter key to create a blank line, center the blank line from the Home tab, and move the object to this line).

With multiple solid two-dimensional AutoShapes on your screen – like circles and rectangles – filled with different colors, arrange them so that they overlap and notice how one blocks out the other. Try changing the order so that a different one appears in the front. The objects are generally layered in the order in which you make them, but you can override this by with the Order tool. In Word 2010, the Selection Pane helps you select objects that are behind other images.

You can also make an image partially transparent so that images behind it show through. You can do this by right-clicking the object and adjusting the transparency level in the Color tab of Format AutoShape (or Object). If you use transparency, you'll want to note the following: The publisher has to manually implement transparency that appears in your PDF file, which may result in color shifts or other problems with formatting your images. If you use transparency, see my tip in the next chapter to avoid this problem.

Insert a textbox. Remove the rectangular outline by changing the line color to no color. Observe how the textbox's fill (the fill is the region inside the textbox) blocks out other drawing objects where they overlap. Remove the fill by changing the fill color to no fill. Notice that the background of the textbox no longer blocks out other drawing objects. The textbox has to be sufficiently wider and taller than the text or some of its text will get clipped. Always check to see that the bottoms of letters like 'g,' which extends further downward, are not cut off (they will be if the textbox is too short).

Compare WordArt to a textbox. A textbox allows you to include text in an arbitrary position in a diagram that easily matches the style of text in the document; you have many of the standard text formatting options in a textbox. WordArt allows for some more artistic formatting. In Word 2003 and 2007 especially, you have to be careful when resizing text so as not to distort the aspect ratio; in Word 2010, change the font size to resize the text without distorting the aspect ratio of WordArt.

Insert WordArt. Enter some text. Try changing the WordArt shape. Explore the effects of adding, removing, and otherwise changing the fill and line colors. Try rotating the WordArt, which is useful for making a spine label for a book cover.

Personally, I prefer to avoid using 3-D style or shadow style, but you may wish to explore these options. I find that I can make a greater variety of 3-D styles or shadows manually than are available here, but I have seen some nice images created with these, too.

The variety of callouts provide comic strip type bubbles. When selected, you can drag the yellow diamond-shape marker, and you can separately move or resize the cloud. Try typing text in the cloud.

If you insert an oval shape, it first looks like a circle. When you resize the oval, you can stretch it into an ellipse. If instead you want it to remain a circle, lock the aspect ratio and stretch it diagonally.

The arc is one of my favorite AutoShapes. You can make a lot of useful curves with this simple tool. It is also useful for labeling angles. Try playing with the arc AutoShape. The yellow markers let you choose the initial and final positions. You can stretch it out so it looks more like a hyperbolic arc, or you can wind it around so it makes a complete circle or ellipse. Try adding a fill color to see what happens.

As an example of the arc tool, try to draw a cylinder. You could draw a circle and use the 3-D option, but if you want to draw modified cylinders, like a coaxial cable, the 3-D option turns out to be less flexible. So another way to draw a cylinder is to make an ellipse, then use the arc to make a semi-ellipse. If you snap objects to the grid and lock their aspect ratios, you can get the ellipse and semi-ellipse to match almost perfectly. Then spread them apart and align them vertically. Add a rectangle, and place it behind the ellipse. Fill all three objects. Remove the outline of the rectangle, and add two horizontal lines at the top and bottom of the rectangle. You may need to adjust the horizontal position of each object a little (without snapping to the grid). There are other ways to draw a cylinder, also. I find this to be pretty flexible: For example, I sometimes need to draw coaxial cylinders, where this works out pretty well. See if you can reproduce the following example.

There are two variations of the line tool that are very useful: freeform and curve. The freeform tool allows you to drag the mouse around like you are drawing with a pencil, but I don't recommend this. Instead, if you use freeform, I suggest you click once at a time to make a polygon-type shape. You can use this, for example, to draw three sides of a cube with different colors (as shown below).

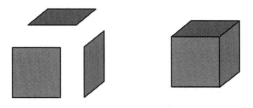

The curve tool can be used to create just about any curved object, which can be open or closed. You can also fill curved paths that you make. I suggest not snapping objects to the grid when you are using the curve tool to give yourself more flexibility. When you first practice using the curve tool, it will probably seem pretty limited. Try using the curve tool to see what I mean, then read the following paragraph.

Make a closed curved path with several points using the curve tool (closed means that the endpoint is coincident with the starting position). If you right-click the image, you will be able to edit the points, add a point, delete a point, or open the path. This allows you to perfect a curve considerably. Explore these options and practice for a while if you want to learn how to create curved drawings that look very professional. Below is a golf hole that was drawn using the curve tool. The other images were drawn using the circle and rectangle tools.

Here is an example that illustrates alignment and rotation. Start with an ellipse. Copy and paste it five times so that you have six ellipses in all. Give them rotation angles of 0°, 60°, 120°, 180°, 240°, and 300°. Align these ellipses two at a time to arrange these ellipses into a rose petal formation. Group these together, then add a circle and center the circle with the group in order to complete the following diagram.

You can also find a host of clipart images, including some available directly from Microsoft. This clipart may not be available for commercial use – you should contact Microsoft or the clipart owner to find out. Some clipart collections do permit commercial use, but some paid collections do not. Always check the documentation to find out; also, you should consult with an attorney for legal advice.

Personally, I find that I can make any image I need, and prefer to do this because it gives me greater flexibility. If I draw a car myself, I find it easy to open a door or add a moonroof because I know exactly what I did to create it. You can edit some clipart images, especially if they are designed for use in Microsoft Word, but you might not find it as easy to make exactly what you want as if you had made the original object yourself. As you draw more and more images, you can develop a personalized clipart collection. All of the images in my self-published books I have drawn from scratch using Microsoft Word (and occasionally Microsoft Excel), except for some of the decorative images used for this book and *Spooky Word Scrambles*, which were designed by artist Melissa Stevens at www.theillustratedauthor.net (I purchased these interior images along with the cover design). The shapes and pictures that you see interspersed throughout this chapter I drew myself in Word.

You can also insert pictures into your Microsoft Word document that were created with other programs. You can add photographs, too. If you are trying to make a specific curve, like a sine wave, you can graph it in Microsoft Excel, remove the outline of the plot as well as the axes and paste just the curve into Microsoft Word.

The possibilities offered by the basic drawing tools in Microsoft Word are virtually limitless (although there are programs, like PhotoShop which can produce professional images efficiently for experienced users, and which also have many possible pitfalls, such as with layers and filters). I wish you success in your endeavors to create professional diagrams.

For your eBook file, all images must be JPEG files with the text wrap set to In Line with Text (not in front of text, behind text, or square). However, images that only consist of line art and text should be GIF images. If you draw a diagram in Word, you can copy and paste it into Paint, for example, to convert it to JPEG or GIF format, although you can get a cleaner image using a more professional graphics program (there are some free graphics programs available, like Gimp).

> Each image must be in JPEG or GIF format for your eBook, placed on a line by itself, with the text wrap set to In Line with Text.

Cover Design and Illustration Resources

- You can find free cover design articles on my blog: www.chrismcmullen.wordpress.com. Once there, click the Cover Design tab.
- Although you can self-publish for free, if you need help, CreateSpace does offer paid cover design and illustration services. From the homepage, click the Books tab, then choose Layout and Design to learn more. Ask if you'll get to keep the cover or illustration file (and in what format), and what happens if you need to make changes after the process is complete. Alternatively, when you reach the cover file upload step when publishing with CreateSpace, you will see a link to learn about using crowdSPRING as a possible cover design service.

- Both CreateSpace and Kindle Direct Publishing offer free Cover Creator tools. These can help you design a basic cover for free. However, the designs are limited, and your cover may look very similar to many other covers.
- It's possible to hire a cover designer. You can find premade covers from $10 to $100, which aren't likely to fit your content perfectly and help attract your target audience as well as a custom cover. You can find custom cover design help from $100 to $300 (and up). I've hired Melissa Stevens (www.theillustratedauthor.net) to design covers, and have been very pleased with the results. Many small publishers who actively participate in the CreateSpace community forum offer their cover design and illustration services. As with shopping for any service, try to learn about the person's character and qualifications, and seek objective opinions from someone who has used the service. View a portfolio of previous work to help judge what to expect. Read your contract carefully. Find out exactly what you're getting for your investment.

7 Preparing the PDF Files

THERE ARE SEVERAL software programs used to produce documents that have text, figures, or both, and these programs can save the documents in different file formats, which have different file extensions (.doc, .txt, .jpg, etc.). Even those files that are written with one program (such as Microsoft Word), yet are saved in a common extension like .txt, may lose features and quality when saved in the more common format. Rather than restricting all authors to use a particular software program, which inherently can not be the best program to produce all types of books that can be written, most print-on-demand self-publishing services ask authors to submit files in a Portable Document Format (PDF). Authors can thus prepare their manuscripts in whichever program they prefer, in principle, and then convert the document to PDF. The conversion of a file to PDF is a means of making it universal – i.e. anyone can open a PDF file on any computer if they have a program that can view a PDF file, even if they don't have the program that was used to write the original document. Acrobat Reader is freely available so that everyone can read PDF files.

Here is the essential idea behind PDF files. Regardless of what program you use to make a document, you are able to print the document by sending the printer a set of instructions for what the document looks like. The printer is not familiar with all of the programs that a computer might use to make documents, which would not be practical. Rather, all programs send a similar set of instructions to the printer to tell the printer what the document looks like. If you can tell a printer what a document looks like, then you can just as well tell a file what a document looks like. So creating a PDF file is sort of like printing to a file, but not quite. If you simply open a document and try to print it to a file, this by itself will not make a PDF file. However, this is the main underlying idea: A PDF file is a universal way of converting a program's document to a file that any computer can view on the screen, even if the computer doesn't have the software program that was used to make the original file.

PDF File

A PDF file is a portable document format that any computer can read (with a PDF reader like Acrobat), which has instructions for how to display the text and figures of a document on a screen, even without knowledge of the software program that was used to prepare the original document.

PDF Conversion Basics

If you have access to a computer that has Microsoft Word 2007 or later and you have prepared a Word document or other text document that was saved in a format with a .docx, .doc, .rtf, or .txt extension, the simplest way to convert the text document to PDF is as follows. However, if your file contains any pictures, this convenient method will decrease the resolution of your images; in that case, it's better to use a different method (such as described later in this section).

- If it is not there already, bring your file to this computer (via CD, floppy disk, or jump drive, for example). It is not necessary to save the file to this computer, but you may.
- Open Microsoft Word 2007 or later.
- Open your file in Microsoft Word.
- Go to Save As and look at the options.
- If the PDF conversion add-on feature has already been installed, choose to Save As PDF.
- Otherwise, where this option would be there will be a link to download and install this option. Do this. It's free and easy: Just follow the instructions, which you will see when you reach Microsoft's website.
- Save your file in PDF format. It may take a couple of minutes, depending upon your file size and the speed of your computer. (If you had to install the PDF conversion add-on, you may need to repeat these steps before you reach the Save As PDF point.)
- If the computer has Acrobat Reader, the PDF file should open automatically. If not, go to where you saved the PDF file and open it manually.
- If the computer does not have Acrobat Reader, you should get this – it's available freely. Search for it with your favorite internet search engine. Look for a website that is clearly part of Adobe's extensive website (it's best to download it from a reliable source).

This is not the only way to prepare a PDF file. There are a myriad of programs available on the web, some free and others not, for converting files of a variety of formats to PDF. I recommend going with a website that you can trust. You should have a reliable antivirus program working before downloading software. Adobe, for example, is one of the major PDF experts, and offers PDF conversion processes (they give you a handful of trials for free).

Some of Adobe's PDF software is relatively expensive (except for Acrobat Reader, which is free) to purchase, but Adobe also offers a conversion service. While there are many free Word-to-PDF converters online, if you prefer to purchase a copy, Nuance PDF Professional is fairly affordable and includes several features. Among the free PDF converters recommended on the Create-Space community forum is DoPDF (I haven't used DoPDF myself, though; I have used the Adobe and Nuance software programs that I've recommended).

If your book includes images, you want to install a Word-to-PDF converter and print the file to PDF. Don't use Word's convenient Save As PDF option. When printing to PDF, explore the options (e.g. you'll probably need to manually change the page size, since the default setting probably won't match the size that you set in Page Layout). Two convenient features to look for in PDF converters are the option to embed fonts and to flatten transparency in pictures.

Don't use Word's convenient Save As PDF feature if your file has images; otherwise, your images may print with a lower than recommended DPI. Instead, install a Word-to-PDF converter and print to PDF.

Although CreateSpace's Guided Setup option allows you to submit a .doc, .docx, or .rtf file, this is not recommended because the formatting of your document is very likely to change. It's better to convert your file to PDF, check the PDF carefully, and submit that.

Beyond the Basics

If you didn't use any features specific to Word 2007 or 2010, you may find the conversion to PDF more reliable by first saving your file with the Word 2003 format (i.e. with a .doc instead of .docx extension). If you used the new equation editor, drawing tools, or other features from Word 2007 and beyond and try to save the file in the 2003 format, those features may not format as well that way; in that case, it's worth trying to maintain the .docx extension. This was a bigger problem in 2007 when the new .docx extension first came out; with Word 2010 and various updates to PDF converters as well as CreateSpace, the conversion to PDF from .docx seems to be smoother (as long as you convert to PDF yourself and upload a PDF file; don't upload a .doc, .docx, or .rtf file to CreateSpace). If you happen to have Word 2007 specifically, the Save As PDF feature might cause some strange formatting issues when trying to do this from a .docx extension (so try installing a PDF converter and printing to PDF instead – something you should do anyway if your file contains images).

Chances are that a basic PDF conversion, such as the one available with Microsoft Word 2007 or 2010, will work just fine for you if your book consists of just text (like a novel). Otherwise, you should look for a PDF converter (there are many available for free online). If you have rather complex images, it's possible that the conversion of your files will involve some technical issues. If so, you might need to seek some expertise with PDF formatting (see the list of resources at the end of this chapter, and first try seeking free help).

CreateSpace will review the PDF files for your cover and book interior and send you an email with their comments. They will tell you if the files are just fine, if they notice minor problems, or if there are major problems that must be corrected. They are very good at identifying problems like insufficient margins, text too close to the page edge, and low-resolution images; but they do not check for formatting, writing, spelling, or grammar issues (those are entirely up to you). If you observe a problem with your proof and ask them about a technical printing issue, they are also very good at understanding your problem and identifying the technical issue(s) that caused the problem. However, CreateSpace is a self-service publisher – i.e. they will only identify the problem for you, but not help you resolve the problem. So if you are unfortunate to have a technical problem, you will have to solve it yourself or look elsewhere for the expertise you need to solve it (unless you invest in CreateSpace's paid formatting or design services). Try posting your question on the CreateSpace community forum; if your question doesn't get answered (most questions posted there, even when highly technical, do get answered) or if you'd like an experienced formatter to help you, many of the small publishers active on the community forum offer paid formatting help.

If you need more than just a basic PDF conversion, you can try one of the many programs or services available on the web. Adobe offers a PDF conversion with many options that are not available when you convert with Microsoft Word 2007 or 2010. They also offer some rather expensive PDF software, which has a ton of detailed features, but again I recommend spending as little as possible when you are starting out. If you use Adobe's web-based conversion, for which you can use for five free conversions, if you explore the options you will see that there are numerous advanced options for formatting your PDF file. You might look into these if you require a specific formatting feature. Alternatively, you might see if a free PDF converter, like DoPDF, can meet your needs.

Following are a couple of problems that I have encountered with my PDF conversions. I am sharing them in case they also apply to you.

If you prepare figures with transparency – i.e. you make the color of an object partially transparent so that objects behind it show through – this may cause a bit of trouble. If you use CreateSpace, they will notify you that your file includes objects with transparency. They manually flatten (that's the jargon) the transparency in your figures, which may cause slight color shifting. If you have rather complex images, the process of manually flattening the transparency might cause the images to come out considerably different than how they appear on the screen.

They recommend flattening the transparency yourself. If you happen to use a PDF conversion program that has a box to check to flatten transparency, this will be convenient; some free PDF converters have this feature. An alternative is to convert your images to JPEG files and insert the JPEG files into your Word document before converting to PDF (depending on the method you use to do this, you might notice stray marks on your images; e.g. using Paint is convenient, but not the best method available).

There are some other issues that are rather common, which are either minor problems or easy to solve. One is that the images in your PDF file might have less resolution than the images in your original document. If the resolution is low, the publisher will let you know that you have figures with low resolution. You can either choose to accept this or try to make them higher resolution. A PDF conversion process that lets you select the desired resolution will help you make higher-resolution images; Microsoft Word's built-in conversion process is very basic, and presently doesn't offer any options (you get options by printing to PDF from Word with a different PDF converter installed, instead of using the Save As feature). Also, be sure to follow the prescription outlined in the previous chapter (following the images of book covers) regarding how to avoid Word's tendency to decrease the resolution of your images.

It may also help if your PDF file has the fonts embedded in the file. If you use common fonts like Times New Roman, Garamond, Georgia, and Calibri, this should not be a problem. If you use rare fonts, you might have to learn how to embed them in the PDF file through the conversion process (provided that the font provider enabled embeddability and that commercial use is permitted by the font license). A PDF conversion program that has embedding options can help you with this. If you're using Word's built-in converter, when you Save As, click Tools, select Save Options, and check the box marked "Embed fonts in the file."

Look your proof over carefully. It might not look exactly the same as your document, or even how your PDF files appear on your screen. The formatting differences could be slight, or they could be substantial, but it's definitely worth looking this over carefully before you make your book available for purchase.

PDF Conversion Resources

- Visit www.adobe.com to get Acrobat Reader to view PDF files. Adobe also offers some paid conversion services. Nuance at www.nuance.com offers a fairly affordable software package, although Adobe is highly regarded by publishers.
- There are several free Word-to-PDF converters available online, such as DoPDF. If you download a file from the internet, be sure to have an updated antivirus program installed on your computer

and check that the site is trustworthy.

- If you need help converting to PDF format, try searching the CreateSpace community help forum and posting your question if you don't find the answer there. Chances are that someone else has had the exact same problem and will be happy to share the solution.
- It is possible to pay a reasonable fee to an experienced formatter if you run into a technical problem and free help and advice don't work out. For example, you might contact one of the experienced small publishers who regularly participate on the CreateSpace community forum. Most of the time, authors can convert their books to PDF format just by taking time to find a suitable converter and asking a question on the forum.

8 Receiving Feedback

F EEDBACK THAT YOU receive from others can be quite valuable. Once your book is available for sale, anybody who reads your book is liable to leave you permanent feedback in a review, so it is worthwhile to receive some feedback prior to this moment and consider any merit that it may have. You know how you view your book. Different people have different views, though, so you want to assess what your target audience might think about your book.

Using Constructive Criticism

Feedback can be useful throughout the production of your book, from when you first conceive of the idea to when you publish your book, and even after your book is on the market. In order to allow yourself to benefit from this feedback, and to handle it well, you must prepare yourself for some constructive criticism. When you request feedback, ask for the reader to give you an honest assessment, and to try to provide comments objectively and tactfully, if possible. Ask them to make comments that are good, not good, and neutral.

People have different views, beliefs, and opinions. What works well for one person may not work well for another. There is not one method of teaching that works best for everyone because different people learn better in different ways: Some learn very well visually, others learn better by speaking and listening; some learn best individually, others learn better in groups; some learn better by participating, others through observation. Similarly, a book style that appeals to one person may not appeal as well to another person.

So some criticism that you might receive may not mean that a certain aspect of the book is necessarily bad – it could just be a matter of a difference of opinion or style, which could appeal to some people better than others. But that doesn't mean you should just dismiss the comment. You really want to know for what percentage of your target audience this works for, and what percentage it does not.

Some who read your book to offer feedback will catch spelling and grammatical mistakes, formatting problems, inconsistencies, organizational problems, conceptual problems, etc. Notes like these will lead to helpful corrections.

You will also receive a variety of other comments and suggestions. Ultimately, you have to decide whether to make revisions based on these comments and suggestions, and to what extent. If you can gauge what percentage of your target audience feels the same way, or otherwise, or is neutral on this point, this may help you in your decision. It's your book, and your vision, so you're in charge and it's your responsibility, but the more your book appeals to your audience, and the wider the audience for your book, the better your sales.

You can receive helpful feedback from close friends and family when you are first developing the concept for your book. You can discuss the concept with them or show them an outline for your book. As you try to share your vision for your work with them, they may provide useful feedback in the early development of your work.

When you finish writing the text for your book, feedback that you may receive at this point is very useful for revisions because the more revisions you make prior to formatting your book for publication, the less hassle you will experience with editing and formatting.

Additional mistakes can be caught, especially those that may have appeared as a result of editing and formatting, when the book interior is complete. Once again, after creating the PDF file, feedback is useful.

When you proofread your own book – which you need to do, since you should have a greater interest in your book than anyone else, and therefore should be more motivated to find mistakes – you sometimes read what you intended to type instead of what you actually typed. Feedback that you receive from others can help you correct mistakes of this sort.

But you want more than just a list of corrections. You also want organizational, stylistic, and conceptual comments and suggestions. You want to know what people think about your book, whether or not it is useful or entertaining, whether or not the book is worth buying, which type of audience may be interested in your work, ideas for improving your book, the quantitative worth of your book, etc.

Feedback is the best way to sample how people will react to reading your book.

If you opt to publish with CreateSpace, you will be able to submit a preview of your book to the CreateSpace community, where you can receive feedback from other authors like yourself. You can also read previews and offer feedback of your own. Another way to receive helpful feedback is to join a writing forum.

Test-Marketing Your Book

When your book is complete and you are ready to publish your work, it may be worthwhile to test-market your book. Distribute copies and solicit some input. This time, you might try to reach a wider audience than close friends and family. If you have a nonfiction book, you could give a presentation and offer some copies to interested readers in exchange for their input (you might even sell pre-publication copies, possibly at a discounted price). If your work is fiction, you could instead hold a storytelling session and similarly distribute copies.

Someone who receives a free or discounted copy and likes your book might help spread the word about your book, which could serve as good promotion for your book. They may appreciate that you asked for their input – people often like to give advice.

You might ask people to make comments in the book itself and return it to you, or just to read it and discuss it with you (and keep the book). You can order inexpensive copies of your book directly from the publisher (if doing this for the purpose of test-marketing, you may not want your book to be available on Amazon.com until later). You might even provide a form with specific questions you would like to have addressed. Whatever method you choose, you would like to receive feedback.

If you're considering investing money in your book at the outset, the results of test-marketing your book can help you decide if the investment may be worthwhile.

If you are able to solicit any good reviews of your book prior to publication, you can include quotes from these reviews on the cover of your book. Include the source of your quote if it is from a magazine or website. Note that you can post editorial reviews on your book's product page through Author Central (see Chapter 10).

Your test-marketing results might be good, and they might not. If they are good, you will have some confidence in your book, and you are ready to publish your book. If the results are not good, it's better to learn this now than later. You have the opportunity to make improvements before publishing your book. The comments, suggestions, and corrections you receive give you the opportunity to revise your book for the better. The next go-around may yield more encouraging results. Believe in your book and go back to the drawing board, if necessary. You might also try presenting your work to a different audience. Maybe others will appreciate your book better than your first sample audience.

Once you develop a fan base (you can create a Facebook page for your book or an email newsletter and provide information about how to sign up at the end of your book), some of your fans may be willing to form a focus group to help provide feedback on your next project (this may also help to build some buzz).

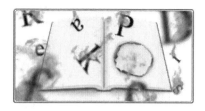

9 Publishing on Amazon.com

ONCE YOU HAVE a completed manuscript, publishing on Amazon.com is easy. One way is to use CreateSpace, a print-on-demand self-publishing company that's part of the Amazon group of companies. If you self-publish with them, you can make your title available for sale directly on Amazon.com as well as through Expanded Distribution channels (which are now free – the cost used to be $25). When your book sells, CreateSpace prints your book and ships it out.

In addition, you can publish an eBook through Kindle Direct Publishing, which will be available for sale on Amazon for Kindle devices (and can also be read with Kindle for PC, iPad, and iPhone). You can also publish your eBook with Nook, Kobo, and other retailers.

If you visit Amazon.com, at the bottom of their home page, you will see a link that says, "Self-Publish with Us." Click this link to learn about how you can publish with Amazon. CreateSpace allows you to publish a paperback to be available on-demand at Amazon (plus Expanded Distribution channels). Kindle Direct Publishing (KDP) allows you to publish a Kindle eBook.

---

www.createspace.com
kdp.amazon.com

Note that your Amazon account will not work at CreateSpace – i.e. you must sign up as a new Create-

Space user. However, your customer Amazon account will work at KDP.

CreateSpace and KDP are not your only self-publishing options. Ingram Spark is a new alternative to CreateSpace. Lightning Source is a more professional option used by many small publishing companies. Some self-published authors also use Lulu. However, Create-Space is a popular option because it's an Amazon company: Many authors trust Amazon through experience or reputation, and it's easy to feed your CreateSpace published paperback into the Amazon sales channel. I have published dozens of books with CreateSpace and recommend it highly (though I still encourage you to do your homework – i.e. compare your options to see what suits your needs best).

You can publish your eBook with Nook, Kobo, and other companies in addition to KDP (unless you enroll in KDP Select, in which case you are choosing to publish your eBook exclusively with Kindle – we'll discuss this option later in the chapter). There are also aggregators like Smashwords and Lulu that help you publish with several eBook retailers at once. I recommend publishing your eBook directly with each retailer when this option is possible – that way, you can view a preview of your eBook directly with the source.

Publishing with CreateSpace

CreateSpace offers softcover book printing. The covers are printed on coverstock and are laminated. You can choose from glossy or matte. They can assign you a free ISBN-10 and EAN-13 and print the ISBN with a UPC bar code on the back of your cover (also free of charge). Alternatively, you can invest $10 to publish with your own publishing imprint.

First, visit CreateSpace's website and setup an account. In order to publish your book and receive royalty payments for sales, you will need to provide information for them to report taxes and bank account information so that they can deposit your royalty checks. They will send you a 1099 after the year ends, reporting your total royalty payments for the year. (Amazon's 1099's are mailed out on January 31, which means you should expect them – you might receive one for CreateSpace, one for KDP, and another for Europe, for example – in the mail one to two weeks into February. You don't want forget and file your taxes before your 1099's arrive.)

Once your account is setup, log in. When you log in, you will come to your Member Dashboard. This is where you can see any books that you are working on or already have published. You can also ask questions here or check your messages (copies of any messages you receive by email). Once you have published a book, you can keep track of your sales on this page (and monitor them more closely with detailed royalty reports). If a book sells on Amazon, you typically see the sale register within 1-2 days on your Member Dashboard (however, there are occasional delays of up to two months).

You should visit the CreateSpace community, where you can interact with other members of the community, such as other authors like yourself, usually through asking or answering questions about self-publishing on CreateSpace. You might also take advantage of the Preview feature, which allows you to make a preview of your book available on CreateSpace. This allows you to obtain feedback from other authors. You can reciprocate by reading other previews and offering feedback.

If you are ready to publish your book, first go to your Member Dashboard, and then click to add a new title. You will see that this is a multi-step process. You may save your progress and continue later (you will probably not be able to do it all at one sitting). Guided Setup is recommended if you're publishing with Create-Space for the first time.

The first step is to enter Title Information. Choose your title and subtitle carefully. These and other fields that are indicated with an asterisk (*) will become permanent when you receive your ISBN.

Here is a tip: Don't enter a publication date. If you enter a publication date, by the time you upload your files, order a proof, revise your proof, and are ready to publish, the date you entered will be weeks in the past. By not entering a publication date, when you press Approve Proof, that date will automatically become your publication date. Why is this important? Because Amazon has new release filters (Last 30 Days and Last 90 Days) that give your book added visibility when it's first published. You get the maximum benefit of the new release filters by not entering a publication date.

Don't enter a publication date. This will give you maximum exposure with the new release filters.

Enter your author information. You can also add coauthors, illustrators, editors, and so on. Anyone who contributed toward your book should be credited for their effort: Some may wish to have their names entered in these fields (if so, their names and roles will also show up next to your author name at the top of the book's Amazon page); others may just wish to be mentioned on the copyright page. If you study traditionally published books, you may note that most only mention cover designers in small print on the back cover and in one note on the copyright page, but not in the contributor fields (fantastic covers often don't mention the cover designer on the front cover).

When your Title Information is complete, save it and move onto the second step. The second step is pretty short: Select an ISBN option carefully. I recommend either free or spending $10 to use your own imprint. If you consider the number of self-published authors and their friends and family, you will see that there is a very large support group for self-publishing. In this way, it's possible for the free option, which will list CreateSpace Independent Publishing Platform in the publisher field, to be more of an advantage than a disadvantage. It depends in part on your genre or content, your target audience, the appearance of your book, etc.

Once you save step two, you will receive your ISBN-10 and EAN-13. I suggest that you add these numbers to the copyright page of your book, if you have such a page. If you had already made your PDF, you will have to make a new PDF file for your book interior after adding the ISBN info to it.

Choose whether to have a black-and-white or color interior. A color interior costs much more. You pay the same price for a color interior whether you have just one page in color or every page in color. Note that your cover can be in color regardless of whether or not the interior is black-and-white. If your interior is black-and-white, you can choose between white or cream pages. Note that different trim sizes have different restrictions on how many pages your book can have, and that this also depends on whether your interior is color or black-and-white; there are also more distribution options if you select one of the "standard" trim sizes. Ensure that your trim size, interior color, and page count match.

The next steps, submitting your interior and cover files, just involve browsing your computer for the PDF files for your book interior and book cover, and selecting and submitting them. (Although you may submit a .doc, .docx, or .rtf file for your book's interior, PDF is highly recommended in order to reduce the chances of significant formatting changes.) Using Interior Reviewer allows you to inspect the live zone and potential problems (but note that some issues that get flagged may not be critical, and Interior Reviewer is not always 100% accurate; if in doubt, proceed to submit your files for review and get a report within 12-24 hours).

You may choose the Cover Creator option if you don't wish to design your own cover. There is also a link to learn about crowdSPRING.

In the next step, you get to review all the information that you have entered thus far. Check this over carefully. When you are happy with everything, submit your book for publishing. Once you do, you won't be able to make any more changes to the steps that you just completed until after someone has reviewed your submission (so if you suddenly realize you need to correct something, you just need to wait about 12-24 hours).

After submitting your files for review, you can proceed to select sales channels, enter pricing information, your book description, and more (you don't need to wait for file review to finish to make *these* changes).

Select your sales channels. The Expanded Distribution channels used to cost $25, but are now free. The Expanded Distribution channel helps to make your book much more visible online (e.g. BN.com, The Book Depository, and many other online retailers are likely to sell your book online). While it makes your book available through some physical channels (like schools and libraries), it's highly unlikely that a bookstore will stock your book by simply adding Expanded Distribution (your best bet is to order author copies to sell to local bookstores directly and approach them with a professional press release kit). Depending on the list price that you have in mind, Expanded Distribution might affect your options to some extent – e.g. it affects the minimum price you can set, so if you were planning on a relatively low list price, you might want to explore this (you can play with the royalty calculator to find out).

The eStore option lets you sell books directly from CreateSpace at a higher royalty rate than Amazon. However, most customers are reluctant to purchase books from CreateSpace because they trust Amazon more, may qualify for free shipping at Amazon, the price is often discounted at Amazon (though you can generate discount codes valid at CreateSpace), and they are required to sign up for an account at CreateSpace. You may also wish to note that sales through your eStore won't affect your Amazon sales rank.

Set the list price for your book in dollars, pounds, and euro. Choosing a good price is not easy. You should check the list prices of competitive titles, complementary titles, related titles, and even CreateSpace titles that seem somehow comparable to your book. If the price is too high, this may discourage shoppers from buying your book. If the price is too low, you make a much smaller royalty.

A lower price will not necessarily result in more sales (in fact, it can even deter sales, as many people believe that you get what you pay for). I explored this with a few of my first books: After reducing the price by a dollar or two, sales were virtually unaffected. But this doesn't mean that you can get away with a high price. There is a limited price range that will seem like an appropriate value. If the price is higher than this, it will discourage sales. If the price is lower than this, it might not improve sales (and might even deter sales).

Another thing to consider is this: What's a fair royalty? The price and royalty go together, so you need to consider both. Publishers often pay a royalty of about 15%. However, publishers also print a large number of books, and expect to sell a large number if they agree to publish your book. If you self-publish, you probably expect to sell fewer books. If you sell fewer books, a somewhat larger royalty may be fair to make it worthwhile to you, financially, to write and publish your book. You're not just an author – you may also be the editor, formatter, cover designer, etc. If you're filling many roles, a higher royalty than a traditional publisher pays just to an author is certainly fair. If you also invest your money for promotional activities, you need to use a portion of your royalties to pay for this.

So it may be fair to earn a royalty that is somewhat greater than 15% of the list price. But you don't want to be greedy, either. If you want a really large royalty, you'll have to make the list price very high, which probably means you'll sell many fewer books and make less revenue from your book.

Keep in mind that you can change the list price once you set it. Shoppers probably won't appreciate it if you raise the list price,[1] but won't mind if you lower the list price. Amazon often discounts the book (but don't worry: if they do this, they pay you the royalty based on the list price, not on the sale price, so it's a good thing). The higher your list price, the more room Amazon has to play with to create a sale price.

Finally, think about what kind of book you are offering. Is it like a mass market paperback, for which there

---

[1] I have actually done this, but I had a good reason. I was selling the first volume of a two-volume set for $11.99. When I published the second volume, I realized how silly this was. Customers buying both would have to pay $23.98 plus shipping. So I raised the price to $12.50 so that buyers would qualify for free Super Saver shipping (back then, Super Saver shipping applied to $25 purchases and CreateSpace paperbacks were rarely discounted; now, there is a good chance that Amazon will discount the list price by 5 to 10% – but pay you the *full* royalty, so it's a good thing – and the minimum purchase for Super Saver shipping has jumped up to $35).

are already numerous popular works available for about five to seven dollars? If so, you will find it difficult to compete at the top of the price range. Is it more like a trade paperback, which can sell for more? (Physically, CreateSpace paperbacks tend to resemble trade paperbacks much more than mass market paperbacks; marketing-wise, CreateSpace authors are also more apt to reach a niche audience than a mass market audience.) Does your book involve expertise that may drive the price up? What is the value of your book? What would you be willing to pay for it? Test-marketing can help you establish a fair value.

Royalties depend on the author cost. Books with a black-and-white interior cost $2.15 for up to 108 pages and $0.85 plus $0.012 per page for longer books. Books with a color interior cost $3.65 for up to 40 pages and $0.85 plus $0.07 per page for longer books.

You receive a 60% royalty, based on your list price, for books sold through Amazon.com, minus the cost of your book. If you sell a book directly through Create-Space, your royalty is 80% minus the author cost. The Expanded Distribution pays 40% minus the author cost.

You receive a direct deposit (if you sign up for it) into your bank account of your royalty payments for a given month near the end of the following month.

Now we'll move onto the book description. Type a description that has up to 4,000 characters (with spaces). Note that shorter descriptions tend to be more effective for fictional works; nonfiction can be somewhat longer if divided into block paragraphs with spaces between or by including bullet points (either you need to learn basic HTML to do this or sign up for Amazon's Author Central – see the resources at the end of the chapter – after you publish; using HTML is better as it will transfer to BN.com, too, but first preview your description in your eStore to ensure that it came out well).

I highly recommend that you first type your description in Microsoft Word and then paste it into the description field later (but if pasting into Author Central, you must first paste into Notepad and then copy/paste from Notepad to Author Central, then reformat in Author Central). For one, Microsoft Word will help you catch spelling or grammatical mistakes. For another, Microsoft Word will let you keep track of how many characters you've used and how many are left.

You want your description to read well, to draw interest to your book, and to help sell your book. Browse other book descriptions on Amazon to get some ideas. Shoppers who come across your book's webpage will probably want to know what your book is about, what it will be like to read your book, and how your book differs from similar titles (without saying negative things about other books or authors). Your description is a sample of your writing, so if it doesn't read well, this might adversely affect your sales. Shoppers might not know that *you* wrote the description, but even so, the quality of the writing of your description can have a positive or negative influence on the customer's first impression.

The next step is to indicate the reading level and enter a category. Note that you have to submit your category, not simply select it. Browse through all of the category options. More than one category will probably apply to your book, so you'll have to choose the best category from the list (but you can contact CreateSpace after you publish to request a second category for Amazon – make a separate request for Amazon UK). You might search for competitive and complementary titles to see what categories they appear in (but the browse categories on Amazon and the BISAC categories listed here are not the same). You must select a children's category at CreateSpace in order to add a second category under "teen" on Amazon (must be done by request).

> If two categories apply to your book, once your book has been published, you may contact CreateSpace to request to have your book added to a second browse category at Amazon.com. Make a separate request for Amazon UK.

You can enter up to five keywords that shoppers might search for on Amazon.com, which relate to your book. A keyword can be a single word or a short group of words (there is a limit for the number of characters, though). I recommend that you not use keywords that already appear in your title or subtitle – words that appear in your title and subtitle may be searchable even if you don't list them as keywords. You will be able to test this out once your book becomes available on Amazon.com (it can take a week after you publish it before you can find it on Amazon), and you can modify these keywords later. Give some thought to what keywords will be useful and appropriate. Bear in mind that shoppers won't be happy if your book shows up in a seemingly unrelated search, so be sure to choose keywords that relate to your book. **See the note in the following section regarding how to use keywords to get your book listed in special categories.**

You can also enter an About the Author section. It's better to sign up for Author Central after you publish and add a biography. If you do both, the biography will show in addition to the About the Author section (and if both are the same, this will seem like a glaring mistake on your product page). Author Central also allows you to easily keep track of sales ranks and reviews, shows you geographic sales data for most of your paperback sales, and has other nice features. Beware that once a paperback book is added to Author Central, it's there permanently (whereas an eBook can be removed by request, once it's unlinked from the paperback edition).

You may receive automatic emails (depending on your account settings) when you create your account, submit your files, revise files, make purchases, and submit your book for publishing. After submitting your book for publishing, within 12-24 hours (usually) you will receive an email from someone who has reviewed your files. This email will let you know if your files are acceptable, and will tell you if there are concerns about the format of your book (like the resolution of your images, or whether the title you entered matches the title of the cover and the book interior); but they won't check for spelling, grammar, writing, or formatting mistakes (those are all up to you).

If your files are unacceptable, you will have to correct the specified problems and resubmit them. If they are acceptable, but they identified concerns, you can either choose to accept your book as it is and continue with the publishing process (it might be best to order a printed proof to see exactly how it looks), or make changes and submit your files again.

Once your files are acceptable and you are content with them, you can order a proof of your book. There are two options for proofing your book – a digital proof and printed proof. I recommend using the Digital Proofer first, and once you're satisfied with that, ordering a printed proof. You really need to have a copy of your printed proof to know exactly what your customers will be getting. Also, you're sure to catch typos in your printed proof that you would miss when viewing the screen.

You will have to place an order for the printed proof, including shipping charges. My proofs *usually* arrive in about a week – faster than the dates that they indicate.

When your proof arrives, review it carefully. Chances are that, no matter how careful you have been and how much feedback you have received, you will spot one or more mistakes. Think of it as Murphy's law if you want. It's important to read through your proof careful-ly, though, since if you choose to approve your proof, this is exactly what you can expect buyers to receive. If there are any mistakes, you want to catch and correct them now. If you do find mistakes, correct them and submit new files, and order a new proof.

Once you have a proof that you are happy with, log-in to your CreateSpace account to approve your proof. You should be able to find your book on Amazon.com within about a week. Check this Amazon page carefully to make sure that there are no mistakes (there shouldn't be, but nobody's perfect).

If you encounter problems or have questions, you can email CreateSpace from your Member Dashboard.

If you need to revise your book after making it available, you can make your book unavailable and go through the process once again to make corrections.

You will probably want to monitor your sales and royalty payments on your Member Dashboard. Once your book sells, you might also want to keep track of your Amazon.com sales rank. Realize that sales fluctu-ate. They will be better sometimes and slower other times. Don't get discouraged if sales start out pretty slow. First, people have to find your book before they can decide to buy your book. Promotional strategies (Chapter 10) can help with this. If sales are slow when your book first hits the market, there is still the hope for sales to increase as awareness of your book grows, and there is the hope that any promotional activities that you might choose to engage in will help increase sales of your book. On the other hand, if sales take off early, there is a chance that they will taper off later.

> Be patient. Give your book a chance and see how things evolve before you judge the success of your book.

Now you should consider promotional strategies. Even if you don't plan to market your book at all (which I don't recommend), I bet you will find a few useful tips in the next chapter and be glad that you read it. ☺

Publishing an eBook

Don't accept CreateSpace's offer to transfer your PDF files to Kindle because PDF files tend to suffer formatting problems when converted to Kindle (but paid conversion services should get you a well-formatted eBook – although you'll learn how to do it yourself in this section). Instead, convert your Word document to eBook format as described in Chapter 5. Then publish your eBook directly with KDP. Simply ignore CreateSpace's offer to transfer your PDF files to Kindle.

After you login to KDP (*not* CreateSpace!), visit your Bookshelf. Click to add a new title.

The box at the top asks if you wish to enroll in KDP Select. If you're not sure, you can leave this box unchecked for now – it's something you can elect to do at any time. However, you can't get out of the program so easily – if you sign up, you must wait for your 90-day enrollment period to end before opting out. Also, enrollment automatically renews, so you must uncheck the box to disable automatic renewal and also wait until the 90-day enrollment period ends in order to opt out of KDP Select.

Since it's not easy to get out of the program, it's important to consider this decision carefully. KDP Select has some enticing benefits. Let me mention the one disadvantage first: If you sign up for KDP Select, your eBook may only be available in Kindle format while it's enrolled in KDP Select. Your eBook can't be available for sale with Nook, Kobo, Sony, Smashwords, your website, or anywhere else in electronic format unless and until your 90-day enrollment period ends (and you have to disable automatic renewal to avoid entering into a subsequent 90-day enrollment). However, you may publish a paperback with CreateSpace and have your eBook enrolled in KDP Select, and you may select the Expanded Distribution channel at CreateSpace (the exclusivity agreement only applies to the electronic edition).

So why would you give up the opportunity to publish your eBook with Nook, Kobo, Sony, and other retailers? Some authors choose to do this because KDP Select does offer some enticing benefits (while other authors prefer not to give up this opportunity):

- You can schedule one Countdown Deal during each 90-day enrollment period. If your eBook price is at least $2.99 in the US (the minimum is £1.93 in the UK), a Countdown Deal lets you create a temporary sale (up to 7 days). Customers will see the list price, sale price, and when the sale ends.

- Instead of a Countdown Deal, you can make your eBook free for up to 5 days per 90-day enrollment period. You don't earn royalties for free eBooks, but this can help you get some early readers. (Personally, I prefer the Countdown Deal, as you're more likely to attract readers from your target audience – plus, you earn a royalty.)

- Amazon Prime members can borrow your eBook. You receive a royalty (usually, about $2, but it varies) for each such borrow.

Should you sign up for KDP Select? It's a tough decision to make. Authors who join KDP Select and receive many sales from Countdown Deals and get many borrows usually stay in the program. Those who don't get much out of the Countdown Deals or borrows often opt out of the program. On the other hand, authors who at first avoid KDP Select who don't sell many eBooks with other retailers often join KDP Select to try it out. The only way to know for sure is try it both ways.

Enter the title exactly the same as you entered it at CreateSpace (use copy/paste). If you entered a subtitle at CreateSpace, include the title and subtitle together in the title field at KDP (separate them with a colon and a single space after the colon). When you add contributors, be sure to spell and punctuate the names exactly the same way (copy/paste them). This way, the paperback and Kindle editions should link together automatically. If they don't link in a few days, use the Contact Us feature at KDP to place a request.

> If your Kindle and paperback editions don't link together on Amazon within a few days, log into KDP, click the Contact Us button, select Product Page, click Linking Print and Kindle Editions, and copy/paste your ISBN and ASIN directly from your product pages.

Enter a description of your eBook. Unlike Create-Space, you can't use HTML in your description at KDP. However, you can edit your description using Author Central (see the resources at the end of this chapter).

As I explained with CreateSpace, I recommend leaving the publication date blank.

Don't use the same ISBN as your CreateSpace paperback when publishing your eBook. Paperback and eBook editions can't use the same ISBN. However, you don't need an ISBN for Kindle: Just leave this field empty and you will receive an ASIN instead.

Similarly, don't enter CreateSpace as the publisher for your eBook. You can either leave this field blank or enter the name of your own publishing imprint, if you have one.

You can select up to 7 keywords at KDP (two more than CreateSpace allows) and two categories. There are some special categories that you can only get in through the use of special keywords. See the link below to a KDP help page that lists the special keywords needed to get your book listed in special categories.

Visit the following KDP help page to learn how to get your book listed in special categories through special keywords (you can use these keywords at CreateSpace, too): https://kdp.amazon.com/help?topicId=A200PDG PEIQX41. Once there, click on one of the categories at the bottom to pull up a table of special keywords.

Select the option to declare your publishing rights. Click the "What's This?" link to learn more.

Upload the image for your cover or use the free Cover Creator option. You can upload a JPEG or TIFF file for your cover. Neither the width nor height may exceed 2500 pixels. Amazon recommends a 5:8 aspect ratio (i.e. the image should be 1.6 times taller than it is wide), in which case the cover would be 1563 x 2500. The thumbnail that you see on Amazon is usually sharper than the sample that you see after you upload your cover. However, it's important to upload a cover that looks sharp and clean full-size because that's how most shoppers will see it when they first look inside your eBook.

Select your preference for Digital Rights Management (DRM). Click the "What's This?" link to learn more about DRM.

Upload the content file for your eBook. If you have images, you should upload a compressed zipped folder (otherwise, you're likely to see subtle formatting problems): Save as a Web Page Filtered, close the file, find the file on your computer (e.g. in My Documents or wherever you saved it), right-click, choose Send To, select Compressed (Zipped) Folder, find the folder with the compressed images (the folder has the same name as the HTML file had), and copy/paste this image folder into the compressed zipped folder.

If you don't have images, you can upload a .doc or .docx file. In the early days of .docx, it seemed that .doc worked better in many ways; recently, I've had better luck with .docx (while many people who recall the early days of .docx continue to advise against it); which is better also depends in part on the nature of your content. If you're not happy with your preview, this is one thing you can try changing to see if it has an impact. (The "pros" will upload an EPUB or HTML file, and will clean and tweak the HTML to perfect subtle features.)

The maximum content file size for Kindle is 50 Mb. If you opt for the 70% royalty option, it's in your financial interest to minimize the file size. If you have pictures, these usually take most of the memory. Compress your images for your eBook file, as explained in Chapter 5, to keep the file size down.

Check your eBook carefully in the preview. Note that there are two previewers. There is a convenient online previewer and there is also a downloadable previewer. The downloadable previewer is more reliable than the convenient online previewer. Check your eBook on all 7 devices: eInk > Paperwhite, eInk > Kindle, eInk > Kindle DX, Fire > Kindle Fire, Fire > Kindle HD, IOS > Kindle for iPad, and IOS > Kindle for iPhone.

It's possible for your eBook to look fine on some devices, but format poorly on one device. The only way to know for sure is to check your eBook carefully on each device. You don't want your customers to be the first to discover any problems.

> Use the downloadable previewer, which is more reliable than the convenient online previewer. Check your eBook carefully on all 7 devices. Even if it looks perfect on a few devices, there may still be major formatting issues on other devices. Resolve any issues before publishing.

On the second page of the publishing process, first select the locations where you have the rights to publish your eBook and set your list prices. Note: If you're enrolled in KDP Select and set the list price at $2.99 in the US, make sure the list price in the UK is at least £1.93, otherwise your book won't be eligible for Countdown Deals in the UK.

The 70% royalty option isn't quite 70%. First subtract the delivery fee from your list price, then multiply by 0.7 to figure your royalty. You don't have to do the math, though: There is a royalty calculator built into page 2 of the publishing process (where you set your list price) that will do the math for you. Under the table that lists the countries, you will find the converted MOBI file size for your Kindle eBook (look below the long table). This determines the delivery fee (multiply by 15 cents in the US). If you have a large file size, it's worth comparing the 35% and 70% royalty options to see which gives you a higher royalty.

The file size affects the minimum list price. If the converted MOBI file size exceeds 10 MB, the minimum list price is $2.99, and if it exceeds 3 MB, the minimum list price is $1.99. You can only set the list price between 99 cents and $1.99 if the file size is under 3 MB.

If you have a paperback edition of this eBook, you may choose to enroll your eBook in MatchBook. This allows you to offer customers an incentive to purchase both your paperback and Kindle editions – the incentive is a discount off your Kindle edition.

The Kindle Book Lending box (not to be confused with KDP Select borrows) will automatically be checked. You can only uncheck this box if you select the 35% royalty rate.

Read the terms and conditions carefully, check this box, and you're ready to publish (maybe you should check everything carefully once more first). Your Kindle eBook should be available in the Amazon US store in about 12 hours (you should receive an email, depending on your account settings).

Check your Kindle product page and explore the Look Inside once your eBook goes live. If you don't have a Kindle, find someone who does who can let you check out exactly how it looks on a Kindle device.

You can revise your eBook at any time (once it goes live). You might want to put a note in the front matter (e.g. the copyright page) so that when you view the Look Inside on Amazon, you'll know which edition you're looking at.

If you don't enroll your eBook in KDP Select, you should also publish your eBook at other sites. The following list will help you get started:

www.nookpress.com
www.kobobooks.com/kobowritinglife
www.smashwords.com

Smashwords can distribute your eBook to Nook, Kobo, Apple, and other retailers. However, an advantage of publishing directly with Nook and Kobo is to see exactly what your preview will look like (if you do publish directly with them, you'll want to disable distribution to these retailers from Smashwords). When you publish at Smashwords, be sure to read the *Smashwords Style Guide* carefully (it's a free guide). Smashwords has other free guides that are also worth reading, such as one on marketing. Smashwords has a few special requirements, like writing "Smashwords Edition" on your copyright page.

Publishing Resources

- You can find free publishing articles on my blog: www.chrismcmullen.wordpress.com. Once there, click one of the following tabs: Cover Design, Blurb, Editing/Formatting, Writing, Marketing, or Publishing.
- Sign up for Amazon's Author Central at https:// authorcentral.amazon.com (for the UK, change .com to .co.uk). You can monitor sales rank and reviews conveniently there, add formatting to your description, and find other helpful features.
- For full-page picture books, you may want to visit the KDP help pages to learn about fixed-layout Kindle eBooks.
- When publishing at Smashwords, read the *Smashwords Style Guide* by Matt Coker carefully before you publish. You can find many helpful free resources on Smashwords' website.
- Although you can self-publish for free, if you need help, CreateSpace does offer paid editing and formatting services. From the homepage, click the Books tab, then choose Editing or Layout and Design to learn more. Ask if you'll get to keep the edited file (and in what format), and what happens if you need to make changes after the process is complete.
- Many small publishers who actively participate in the CreateSpace community forum offer their editing and formatting services. As with shopping for any service, try to learn about the per-

son's character and qualifications, and seek objective opinions from someone who has used the service. Ask to have a sample chapter edited or formatted as a token of what to expect. Read your contract carefully. Find out exactly what you're getting for your investment.

- Amazon has a free guide for basic Kindle formatting called *Building Your Book for Kindle*. You can read it on a PC or Mac.
- If you need help with formatting issues, for paperback help, try searching the CreateSpace community help forum and posting your question if you don't find the answer there, and for Kindle help, try using the Kindle community help forum. Chances are that someone else has had the exact same problem and will be happy to share the solution.
- The Kindle help pages (see the link below) have many useful tips.

https://kdp.amazon.com
/help?topicId=A3R2IZDC42DJW6

- It is possible to pay someone to format your Kindle eBook for you. CreateSpace offers this service. While you shouldn't accept the free offer to send your PDF to Kindle (because PDF's tend to format poorly as eBooks), their paid services will result in an actual eBook format, not a PDF. Alternatively, Kindle lists a variety of companies who specialize in Kindle conversion services (see the link below):

https://kdp.amazon.com
/help?topicId=A3RRQXI478DDG7

10 Marketing Strategies

MARKETING HAS TWO sides. On the one hand, promotional strategies help authors spread awareness of their work, reaching more customers and, hopefully, increasing sales of their books. This is also beneficial to your target audience: Someone who might not otherwise have known about your book who buys and reads your book, and who enjoys your book or draws usefulness from your book, similarly benefits from your effort to market your book.

As I have said all along, I recommend not investing much in your book until your book starts to sell and you establish some measure of how well your book is selling. By using part of your royalties to invest in promotional activities, you can stay in the positive as you undertake such tasks. Also, by being patient this way, when you finally do some work to promote your book, you will be able to see firsthand what effect, if any, it may have had on your sales. This way you can see what is or isn't worth trying again so that you put investments where they are most effective.

Two places where it might be worth investing initially are cover design and editing. If you have friends and acquaintances with some measure of editing skills, they might be able to help you catch mistakes and offer valuable feedback. You definitely need a second pair of eyes to read your book because the author very often sees what he or she meant to write instead of what is actually written (you can gain a pair of ears using text-to-speech – this can help you catch phrases that sound funny to your ear).

Cover design is an important part of your marketing: The cover should quickly show the target audience that this book is for them. Your cover is also part of your branding process. If you have a highly marketable book (that's a big 'IF'), paying for a cover that attracts your target audience may pay off. (This requires the content to appeal to the audience, the cover to succeed at its job, and the description and Look Inside to be effective.)

Your book's description and Look Inside are also important aspects of your marketing. Only a fraction of the potential customers who view your book on Amazon will actually make a purchase. The effectiveness of your description and the quality of your Look Inside are huge factors. The description needs to concisely convey what to expect without giving too much away, and it needs to create interest in your book. The Look Inside needs to look professional, read well, and engage interest. It's worth studying top-selling books similar to yours to learn how to write effective blurbs and what a professional Look Inside looks like (especially, find blurbs of top-selling books that aren't selling because of the author's or publisher's big name).

The content is another huge factor in your marketing. Once customers read your book, the quality of the content will determine whether or not they recommend your book to others. This can come in the form of reviews and word-of-mouth sales. When customers spread news about your book through conversations, this is among the best marketing you can get. It's also the hardest marketing to get because the quality of your book must earn it. People read many average and good books without recommending them. It takes something special, like a book that moves them emotionally or a character they fall in love with to do this. Editing and formatting factor into this, too, because it's harder to recommend a book that has many mistakes in it.

The most effective marketing you can do tends to be free. Most authors struggle with marketing because they don't really know what to do or don't want to take the time to learn and try out ideas (and most of the ideas don't yield immediate results, but take months of patience). The result is that many authors are hoping to throw some money at marketing to get it to work, but it doesn't work that way.

Why does free book marketing tend to be better than paid marketing? Because personal interactions are a huge part of book marketing. You meet people at readings or signings, social media, and most of your online and offline marketing endeavors. Other people (e.g. publicists) can help arrange events for you, but *you* are the person who will have to make the appearance and do the bulk of the "work" involved in marketing anyway.

When people see your passion firsthand, have a chance to judge your character, realize that they share commonalities with you, and experience your charm, for example, such things can significantly improve your chances of creating interest in your book. When you look at the reasons that people by books (such as browsing bestsellers, recommendations, also bought lists, and keyword searches), one reason that may be most effective for independent authors is personal interactions with the author. Nobody else can do this for you. You're selling (and branding) yourself in addition your book.

Many of the free and low-cost things that you can do to market your books are easy to set up and just require putting a little time into them here and there over a long period of time. You don't build a professional author platform overnight, but you don't need to try. Develop it slowly over a long period of time and your platform and following will both grow and have substance.

Time is on your side. A little here, a little there is all it takes... if you keep it up. Focus on what you can have several months down the line. Don't dwell on what you don't have today. Don't expect instant results. A following and fan base can start out very tiny and grow very slowly, but if you have continued growth, a time can come – often many months down the line – where it begins to accelerate. It often pays to be very patient.

Another thing that can help significantly in the long run is having several similar books. When you market a handful of similar books, some customers will buy multiple books. Some customers will buy one book today, and if they like it, will check out your other books in the future. Amazon may show your new books to previous customers, and some will check them out. Every new book that you release gives you additional exposure in the new release categories. Just having multiple titles published over a period of time shows readers that you're a serious author: If they like your book, there is plenty more where that came from.

So don't let your marketing efforts detract from writing more books. Put most of your time into writing, but put some regular time into marketing. Don't worry about perfecting your marketing in the beginning. Focus on gradually building a professional author platform step-by-step. Work on one step here, one step there, thinking how each step can be part of something much bigger several months down the line. You're not marketing for instant sales (though any of those are a sweet bonus) – set your sites on a successful future.

Marketing with Little or no Cost

It's a common mistake for authors to "hope" that they won't need to market their books. Then after they release their books, when sales are very slow, they realize that marketing is an important factor. But then it's too late. Why is it too late? Because of how sales rank works.

Amazon's sales rank is a combination of daily, weekly, and monthly sales. If your book has scarcely sold in the past month and suddenly sells today, its sales rank drops to about 100,000 and then starts climbing rapidly. If another book has sold steadily this month, but suddenly stopped selling today, its sales rank climbs much more slowly. A history of slow sales works against you, while a history of frequent sales helps you.

Sales rank factors into some customers' buying decisions (not everyone knows about sales rank and not everyone wants to buy what's "trending now," but it is important to a significant number of customers). Sales rank also affects your book's visibility on Amazon in various ways. The more sales you get, the more you benefit from Customers Also Bought lists and other forms of Amazon marketing.

What does this mean? It means that authors who hope to avoid marketing, but learn the hard way that they must learn how to market their books are sort of shooting themselves in their feet, so to speak. It's easier to try to maintain a history of frequent sales than it is to overcome a history of slow sales.

The solution is simple: It's called premarketing. If your book is ready to publish today, don't. Wait a few months. Unless you have time-sensitive nonfiction information, you *can* wait a few months. This will give you time to do some premarketing; you can use this time for extra editing; and also use this time to start working on your next project.

You can do effective premarketing by just spending a little time each day on the following activities. You don't need to build Rome in one day. Spread it out. The main thing is to start early and accomplish a little of the work each week. A nice thing about premarketing is that it will make an easy transition to marketing. Remember, you want writing your next book and perfecting your current book to be your main priorities, but you also want to squeeze a little time for marketing into your weekly activities. Here are some premarketing ideas:

- Strive to build buzz about your book. Keep friends, family, acquaintances, and coworkers informed about the progress of your book so they look forward to it. Every time you solicit feedback (even a simple cover reveal), it's an opportunity to create more interest.

- Start a blog months before you publish for two reasons: (1) It helps you build a small following that might lead to a couple of sales and (2) when you direct readers to your blog, there will be some content there instead of an empty blog.

- Create an author page and/or book page at Facebook. You can feed a WordPress blog into a Facebook author page, so you don't need to make separate posts for the two sites. You can also feed your blog into Twitter (but don't feed between Twitter and Facebook or you'll get double posts).

- Prepare for a fan club. The main site for this could be your Facebook author page or it could be a page from your blog. Find an email subscription service that will let you begin an email newsletter for your fan club.

- Create an about the author page for the back matter of your book. Include the url to your blog, Facebook author/book page, and Twitter page. Include the email to subscribe to your fan club.

- Order business cards or bookmarks. When you interact with people personally and mention your book, pass out a business card or bookmark.

- Find bloggers who share a similar target audience who may be interested in reading and reviewing your book. You can also give review copies to people you know. (If you give out a free copy in exchange for a review, the reviewer is required to state this in the review.)
- Try to generate early sales from people you know both in person and online (e.g. Facebook).

Your hope is that premarketing will stimulate some initial sales and that regular sales will follow. If your premarketing and packaging (cover, description, and Look Inside) are effective and your content is excellent, that's what *should* happen. But even if sales turn out to be fairly slow at first, don't panic. For one, your premarketing has given you a headstart toward building a professional author platform. You might solicit feedback on your packaging and content. However, the bigger factor may be that it takes time to get discovered.

On Amazon, your book is just one of millions. It's hard for new books to get discovered there. Your book will show up at the bottom of search results and won't appear on any Customers Also Bought lists until customers find and purchase your book. With effective marketing, you can improve your book's discoverability, but it still takes time. It won't change overnight.

Marketing tends to start out very slowly. When you first setup your blog, you get a few followers and a little traffic, and may not even get any direct sales from it. Social media followings develop slowly and many of the followers may be outside your target audience. Don't focus on how slow things start. Set your sights on what they might become over the course of several months.

One of your online goals should be to develop a content-rich website that will attract your target audience. Start out with a simple blog and work your way toward transforming it into a content-rich website. A blog is something easy to do and appeals to writers because it involves writing, but a content-rich website that attracts people who aren't already fans or followers can be a highly effective marketing tool.

You can't start out with a content-rich website because it takes time to develop the content. What you can do is create a little content here and there over the course of several months for your blog.

I recommend WordPress: www.wordpress.com. The .com site is a free and easy way to create a blog website. You don't need to know HTML or anything about web development. (Those with expertise in these areas might want to look into the .org site.) I've used BlogSpot, too, but had much better success with WordPress.

If you mostly blog about yourself, this won't attract new readers. If you blog short stories, you'll probably discover that it's no easier to give them away than it is to sell them on Amazon. What you want to do is create nonfiction content that will attract your target audience – i.e. it needs to relate to the content of your book, even if it's a novel. It's very important that your website and book share the same target audience. You can occasionally post something personal, which helps to show that you're human and reveal your character, but if you mostly post about yourself, your blog won't serve as an effective marketing tool (unless you're a celebrity).

When you post your first few nonfiction articles, hoping to attract your target audience to your blog, you'll probably be very disappointed. It's not easy to get discovered, especially in the beginning. You have to think long-term. Initially, you have very little content to attract anybody and your blog has had very little time to get noticed. Things generally start out very slowly.

If you just post one article every week or so, you can still put most of your writing toward your next book, and eventually you will have a content-rich website and your blog will start to get noticed more. Mention your book at the bottom of each of your posts, with a link to your book's product page at Amazon (it may not lead to any sales in the short-term – think long-term). Include a relevant image that will attract interest in your article. Test out relevant keywords on Google: Ideally, these will be specific to your article, searched for frequently, but not so popular that your article won't be found.

In the beginning, each post may get a dozen views, a handful of likes, and a couple of followers. This will help to slowly grow a following. What's more important is getting a few articles discovered through search engines. This takes planning and much patience. Learning about search engine optimization (SEO) can help to some extent, but ultimately it's the quality and value of the content that you write that makes the difference. Even if you write novels, you want to think about nonfiction content that you can create that will help to attract your target audience through search engines.

After a few months, you might have a humble following of 50 or 100 followers, you might get a couple dozen views of your posts, and you might have a dozen or more likes of each post. You'd like these numbers to grow over time as it's a show of support, but these aren't the stats you should worry about. For one, only a fraction of your followers will actually read your posts and only a fraction of those are in your target audience. Focus on reaching people beyond your blog. The external traffic that checks out your old posts are the more important numbers. Many months from now, once you have several content articles, you can add a page to your blog that serves as a table of contents or index.

If you view your WordPress stats and see posts from weeks ago getting a few views per day, you're headed in the right direction. After several months, you might have a dozen or more older posts that get an average of 1-10 visitors per day. If one year from now, you have 50 or so people discovering your blog each day through search engines, that's a lot of traffic (multiply this by 365 – that's 18,000 visitors per year).

The goal of your blog should be to gain discovery through search engines from your target audience. It can take several months to reach this point. If you see activity on older posts and if you see that your blog is being discovered through search engines, this is a positive sign. If these numbers (not the likes and follows) grow a little each month, things are going well. If not, you need to reevaluate your content.

You can also try to publish an article with a high-traffic website, online magazine, print magazine, newspaper, etc., in addition to your blog. Really, you have nothing to lose: In the worst-case that nobody accepts it, you can still publish your article on your blog. However, there are so many websites out there, you have good prospects for getting an article posted where there is moderate traffic. The main thing is to submit to places that share the same target audience. If you get your article accepted and list Your Name, author of Your Book at the end of your article, this can lend you some helpful exposure and help to build credibility.

Your blog isn't just about developing a content-rich website. Interactions and connections are valuable parts of your blogging. Visit other blogs, meet other authors, find editors and designers, and interact with people in the comments sections. When you visit other blogs, you'll get ideas for things you could be doing. When you interact with other authors, you'll share tips and develop a support network. You'll make connections that may prove valuable in the future. You can mix in occasional fun posts, try out a new writing style, show a little of your personal side, or spread some goodness, and you'll enjoy the writing variety that a blog offers (but you want most posts to provide valuable content).

You also want to take advantage of the benefits of social media. This was huge when self-publishing started, but the tide is turning toward content-rich websites. Still, you want to have both. There are many people who love Facebook and Twitter, so you'll get some followers if you simply have a presence there.

This doesn't necessarily mean more work. The simple thing to do is feed your WordPress posts into your Twitter and Facebook pages. Create a Facebook author page (you can do it from your personal profile – it's not a separate account) and feed your blog posts into that instead of your personal profile. But don't feed posts between Twitter and Facebook (they will both invite you to do this) or you'll wind up making double or triple posts, which will deter followers.

You might want to do something different for your fans. People who have read your book might want to learn more about the characters, read about your work in progress, find supplemental content from the book, learn about promotional pricing for your new release, and learn a little more about you as a person. People who haven't read your book want to find valuable content and might want to know about a promotional price for the first book in a series. These are two separate audiences. You might want to have a fan page or book page (at Facebook, for example) dedicated just to fans, and a content-rich website to attract new readers. This requires a little extra work, but may be worth it. Your fan base will pay off when you notify them about your upcoming book.

An email newsletter offers something that your blog and social media don't do: It provides an effective filter. Most of your followers don't read your posts or aren't in your target audience. Most people who subscribe to an email newsletter have some interest in the content. This means you have to send out an occasional email with content that will interest your target audience. You can give away a free PDF booklet, for example, as an incentive to subscribe to the newsletter. If your newsletter provides valuable, engaging content, you can grow a following that will actually read what you have to say. You don't have to spend too much time on this: A bi-weekly or monthly newsletter is easy for you to keep up with, and won't feel like spam to your readers. You must provide an unsubscribe option with your email (many email subscription services will do this for you).

Another thing you should work on is a press release (PR) kit. This will be useful for approaching bookstores, libraries, local newspapers, local radio stations, and potential reviewers, for example. A press release kit includes a press release announcement, a cover letter (which needs to fit each occasion), a business card, a tip sheet, a copy of your book, and a sales sheet with relevant sales data and review excerpts (sales and editorial reviews being pertinent to bookstores and libraries – you won't include this sheet where it's not pertinent).

You can post your PR kit on a page on your website, too. When your PR kit is relevant for online interactions (like trying to get news coverage online or seeking online reviews), you can include a link to your online PR kit. (You won't include a copy of your book on your website, but if you have an eBook, you can gift it or attach it to an email – but don't send files via email without prior consent from the recipient.)

There is a prescription for how to write a press release announcement. Anyone in the media or bookstore relations is familiar with this. So if you don't follow the convention, it will stand out like a sore thumb. I recommend reading *Get Your Book in the News: How to Write a Press Release that Announces Your Book* by

Sandra Beckwith, a former publicist. It guides you step-by-step through the process and includes examples (also check out Sandra's press release on her website – some formatting comes out better there than it does in eBook format – www.buildbookbuzz.com; this also serves as a good example of a content-rich website and an effective email newsletter).

Your PR kit is a tool that can help you get your book stocked in local bookstores or libraries, help you get your book in the news (in print, on the air, and online), and help to solicit book reviews through review copies. Start small and local and work your way outward.

Your best chance to get your book stocked in bookstores is to approach small, local bookstores (and other stores that sell books in addition to other merchandise) in person with your press release kit, including a copy of your book (have more nicely packed in your car). They don't want to order your book through Ingram (via the Expanded Distribution channel) or through CreateSpace Direct (also through the Expanded Distribution channel) because your book won't be returnable or have a sufficient discount. Chain bookstores probably won't stock your book nationally, but local stores may work with you.

You can offer 40 to 55% off the list price by selling author copies. It would be ideal for you to sell copies to the bookstore, but the bookstore is more likely to want consignment. It's a negotiation. Try to sell your book at 40% off, but be willing to go up to 55% and be willing to settle for consignment. Some authors specify something like 45% off for consignment, 55% off for purchase, giving an incentive to avoid consignment; but be willing to settle for what you can get.

Personal interactions are one of a self-published author's best marketing assets. Even in this age where there are hundreds of thousands of authors, it's still cool to be able to say you've actually met the author of a book. When you meet people, let them discover that you're an author, rather than advertising this. People usually don't like advertisements, like, "Hey, I just published a book," but they like to make discoveries, like when they ask you, "What do you do?"

You can interact with people at readings, signings, following presentations, at conventions, in community service, and many other ways that you can involve yourself with activities where you're likely to meet and interact with your target audience. Show professionalism, reveal your passion for writing and your topic, and charm your potential readers. A significant percentage of books are purchased by readers who had previously interacted with the author and enjoyed the meeting. You can interact with more people online, but personal interactions are much more meaningful and can make a more lasting impression. Readings, presentations, workshops, and seminars allow you to sell copies in person when the event ends.

Branding is an important marketing concept. It's the idea behind commercials and billboards. If you see an advertisement, you don't run to the store immediately and buy the product. Rather, the advertisement brands a name, image, or idea. Months later when you're shopping, you see a few brands to choose from, and you think things like, "I've never heard of this," and, "I recognize this brand."

Advertising doesn't tend to be effective for books, except in special circumstances like promoting a special sale price (and even then it may not pay off). Unlike advertising a brand of coffee where there aren't many to choose from, there are millions of different books on the market. But you don't need paid advertising.

You can achieve the effect of branding for free. Every time someone in your target audience sees your cover, sees your author photo, or hears or reads your name, for example, you are branding the image of you or your book. The more exposure you get, the more readers will recognize your brand when shopping for a book.

Marketing very often doesn't result in an immediate sale, but works through branding. For example, when people read your online posts and see your name at the bottom as the author of a book, they probably won't go straight there and buy it, but they might recognize your book sometime in the future.

Branding requires patience. A potential customer might see your book, photo, or name once today, again in a month, and once more a few months from now, then recognize your book a few months after that while shopping. Hence, it can take months of active marketing for branding to show its effects. Don't dwell on short-term sales; build for long-term potential (but do analyze your marketing strategies, seek feedback, and try to improve your marketing effectiveness).

Strive to brand a professional image as an author; positive branding is far more likely to result in sales than negative branding. Also, you want exposure, but not to seem like an advertisement – i.e. you don't want to get tuned out (like repeatedly announcing your book through social media).

Finally, let's consider your book's product page on Amazon. I recommend that you buy a copy of your own book on Amazon.com. You can buy a copy cheaper through CreateSpace, but you should still buy one from Amazon. After you buy your book, you can see how long it takes for your royalty to show up at CreateSpace.[2] You

---

[2] Well, occasionally a royalty can be delayed by a couple of months. Once you get your book, if the royalty doesn't show up for several days, contact CreateSpace with the printing numbers from the last page and ask if they can track the royalty for you.

will see how this affects your sales rank. By the way, with a better sales rank, your book shows up sooner on a search sorted by Bestselling. Plus, you can double-check that books bought through Amazon.com are, in fact, identical to your proof copy (except, of course, that your proof copy has the word "PROOF" written on the last page).[3] Finally, it's nice to have a memento of your self-published book.

Beware

It is against Amazon's policies for anyone who has a financial interest in the book to review it. This includes the author, household family members (e.g. spouse, children, or parents), as well as editors, agents, and publishers. These people are <u>not</u> allowed to review your book on Amazon.

If a review is posted that violates Amazon's policy, it will be removed (if not immediately, eventually). Abuse of the customer review policy can lead to account suspensions, removal of the book, and even revoking the right to sell on Amazon. Some reviews are also removed that may not seem to violate the policies. For example, if a friend reviews your book, it's possible that the review won't show up or that it will be removed later. Amazon compares IP addresses, shipping addresses, and other data in their customer and author databases, and any matches will likely block reviews from showing up.

---

[3] I did this once and the book bought through Amazon actually had some formatting errors that my proof did not have. I contacted CreateSpace. They replied, corrected the problem, and apologized. Fortunately, I was the first customer, and no other copies had been sold yet. I was glad that I had bought a copy. They said that it was a very rare occurrence. It hasn't happened again with any of my other books, so I believe them. It's worth the peace of mind to check.

Never let a customer review a book from your computer; if you and a customer have ever logged into Amazon from the same computer, or if you've ever shipped a gift from Amazon to the customer, the review is likely to be blocked. When authors do review swaps, the reviews may be removed. I'm not asking if you agree with this (Amazon isn't asking us, either), I'm just letting you know it might happen so you're not surprised. ☺

When you are next in the market for a book, you might see if there is a suitable self-published book for your needs. Support your fellow self-published authors when possible. Don't do this blindly: Make sure that the book does suit your needs, and check that it looks well-written and has good reviews. Reward self-published authors who produce quality books. The more good self-published books there are, the better image self-publishing will have. If you enjoy a self-published book, or find it useful, please write them a favorable review and explain what you liked about the book – the authors will greatly appreciate your effort.

Amazon reviews can be hard to get. For some books, it takes an average of 500 books or so to get one review. It depends on the genre and content. There are books that tend to get more reviews, such as the one you're reading now. Most of the readers of this book are self-published authors, and nobody understands the importance of reviews better than us. As of February, 2014, this book has received 41 reviews (and I'm thankful for each and every one). I didn't ask anyone for a review, and none are from friends or family: The best reviews are the ones that come naturally from customers.

It may be tempting to recruit reviews, but what you really want is honest feedback. Friends and family are more likely to post five-star reviews that really don't say anything useful ("This book was awesome," isn't helpful to shoppers), and they're also likely to be blocked or removed by Amazon. If you write a five-star review for a fellow author and ask for one in return, it will be hard for that author to be honest (if he or she doesn't like your book, do you think he or she will really leave a two-star review after you just left a five-star review?), and again Amazon may remove the reviews. You're not allowed to pay for reviews – that's against Amazon's policy (however, you may give a free book – but nothing more – in exchange for a review).

Publishers typically send out several advance review copies, hoping to generate some early reviews. You can do this, too, but if you wind up with a dozen reviews and a sales rank indicative of virtually no sales, customers who notice this may be suspicious.

The best thing you can do to generate reviews is to generate sales through quality content, effective packaging (cover, description, and Look Inside), and effective marketing. The natural reviews that you get from actual readers who don't know you and who take the time to leave an assortment of honest feedback is best. They come about slowly, but that's okay – this way, the number of reviews is more likely to match your sales rank.

Every book has strengths and weaknesses. Even if you just look at the writing style, no writing style pleases everybody. Find the most highly rated books of all time and you can find hundreds of people who feel that they were horribly written. That's because no writing style appeals to everyone. For example, many readers like writing to be easily understood, but some want the ideas to be expressed with complexity – there is no way to please both audiences with the same book.

This means that your book has strengths and weaknesses, too. A balance of honest opinions will reflect both your book's strengths and its weaknesses. If grammar is one of your weaknesses and a review exposes this, don't fret about it. The review is helping customers who value grammar highly, but won't deter customers for whom it's not as important as a great storyline or wonderful characterization. On the other hand, you can get your book edited and note this in the description, and then customers who value grammar won't be deterred (ideally, you would have your book edited before getting a review that complains about this).

Any review that doesn't provide an explanation is essentially worthless – it's affecting your average star-rating, but won't matter to customers who read the reviews. If a review says, "The story is wonderful," or says, "This book stinks," but doesn't explain why, customers will simply ignore those reviews – they aren't helpful. You'll get some reviews that don't have explanations; just realize that they won't factor into purchase decisions. What reviewers say is more important than the number of stars. Interested shoppers will also inspect the Look Inside to see if it agrees with reviews. For example, if the review says that the book is well-written or horribly written, checking out the first few paragraphs can easily show if the review has merit.

Having all four- and five-star reviews might make you feel good inside, but might seem suspicious to customers. It's possible that you'll have mostly good reviews. In fact, if most of your reviews come from customers who personally interacted with you during your marketing endeavors, this is quite likely. Customers don't know how the reviews came about, but they do know that authors have abused the system in the past (they also don't realize that Amazon has cracked down on this and made it much more difficult to abuse the system in recent years). Many customers assume that the first reviews are written by friends and family.

On the other hand, getting a one- or two-star may not deter sales. In some circumstances, it can actually help sales (though you'd be a fool to *try* to get a negative review – unfortunately, these come enough without any help at all). A negative review is more likely to affect sales if you don't have other good reviews to balance it or if it exposes a problem that's important to your target audience (in which case, you might address that problem with a revision and note it in the description).

It's really tempting to comment on reviews, but very wise to avoid this temptation. Some customers feel very strongly that reviews are for customers and authors should stay out of this space (*these* customers don't buy books when they see comments from the author).

The last thing you want to do is comment on a review and show your frustration or otherwise react emotionally and ruin your reputation as an author. If you do comment on a review, you must do so tactfully, but even then it's better not to comment at all. If the review was left by a spiteful individual, your comment is just inviting more spite. Guess what the reviewer will do: He or she will ask you a question in his or her response to your comment. Now you have to answer the question, right? Pretty soon, what you intended to be a single comment turns in to a discussion with several comments. It just doesn't look good to customers. Instead, by not commenting, you show that you're a professional author.[4]

Another Amazon feature that may interest you is how search results work. Customers search for books by keywords and by category. Choose the most relevant categories and keywords for your book to benefit from these searches. When customers search for your book, click on your book, and purchase your book, this helps to improve your book's visibility; and sales rank factors into search results to some extent.

---

[4] I have commented on a few reviews, and I've seen many other authors attempt this (sometimes unsuccessfully). The best that can happen may not offset the risk of the worst that can happen.

Sign up for an account at Amazon's Author Central (https://authorcentral.amazon.com and change .com to .co.uk for the UK) and you can add your biography and photo to your book's product page. Author Central lets you add basic formatting to your description, add other sections to your product page, quickly see sales rank and recent reviews, and has other cool features. For example, you can feed your blog posts into Author Central.

Other Promotional Opportunities

I'm a light promoter myself. I appreciate the aesthetic value of having completed the task of preparing a professional-looking book, and I'm happy just to have my work available to those who might be interested in it. I'm content with regular sales, but don't feel a need to be a bestseller. I do give copies of books to my students, occasionally – e.g. when they earn high scores on exams. I have also donated some copies of my books to the school where I teach, for my students to use as part of their course (I make problem sets and laboratory manuals in physics, for example, in addition to my other books). I write because I enjoy it, not for a living.

I do market my books with a content-rich website, but I do this to provide free resources to other authors and to share my passion to be part of the indie-publishing revolution, not to boost sales (that's just a sweet bonus). I interact with people in my target audience, but again it's about helping others, not generating sales (though I'm happy with any sales, of course). I don't do much in the way of promotion, like advertising or contests.

You may be able to motivate yourself to market your books with a similar approach. If you write with passion, but don't write with royalties as your main goal, motivate yourself to market your books as a way to share your passion.

I do have a little experience with advertising and click-through rates from promoting a special event that I created called Read Tuesday. This is a special sales event in December, similar to Black Friday but just for books (you can check it out at www.readtuesday.com). I started this to help promote reading and literacy, and to create a promotional opportunity for indie authors (you're welcome to participate – at no cost to you).

One thing you might do to help promote your book is create a temporary sale price. Kindle has a tool that can help you do this for your eBook: If you participate in KDP Select, you can do a Countdown Deal (if your list price is at least $2.99). If you're not in Select, you can simply lower your price temporarily (unless your price is already at its minimum).

Prices don't sell books. You need to promote a sale for it to be effective. This means you need to spread the news about your sale price to your target audience. Just posting this on your blog may not help much, especially if most of the traffic comes from people who already know about your book. You might be able to find bloggers who share the same target audience who are willing to announce your sale. There are also some popular reader websites that may be willing to advertise your book's sale (see the resources at the end of the chapter).

Another way to generate a little interest in your book is through a giveaway or contest. For example, Goodreads has a giveaway program, or you might look into Rafflecopter. You must promote the contest effectively to get the most out of it.

One kind of contest is to give away a bookmark, book, or related item. Another kind of contest is to enter a writing competition like the Amazon Breakthrough Novel Award. There are many contests open to self-published books. If you get into the later stages of a contest, this may give you some nice exposure.

Authors who write series have additional tools at their disposal. Some price the first book cheap (or even free, through price-matching – i.e. they make the price free at another retailer like Kobo or Smashwords, get customers to notify Amazon about the cheaper price, and succeed in making their eBooks permanently free), while others create an omnibus at an enticing price to encourage the sale of multiple volumes at once.

Fiction books may get significant sales in audio book format. This entails a large upfront cost, but there is less competition among audio books (and there is an audience, e.g. truck drivers). The Audiobook Creation Exchange (ACX) is an Amazon platform mentioned in the KDP newsletter.

What's best? That's the million-dollar question, and varies from author to author and book to book. A few things that have much potential for most authors are content-rich websites, personal interactions, and writing more similar books with highly marketable content. The best thing is to do a little here and there, explore different options, and strive to build a successful future.

* * *

I hope that this book has been useful to you, and wish you the best regards in your writing and publishing endeavors. Thank you, kindly, for reading my book.

Marketing Resources

- You can find free marketing articles on my blog: www.chrismcmullen.wordpress.com. Once there, click on the marketing tab.

- CreateSpace offers both free and paid marketing resources. From the homepage, click the Free Publishing Resources tab. For paid resources, click the Books tab, then choose Editing or Layout and Design to learn more.
- Visit www.buildbookbuzz.com to see a website maintained by a former publicist. It's a good model for a content-rich website, an effective subscription newsletter, and how to write a press release announcement. There are some free marketing resources on this website (in addition to some paid services).
- Here is a sample of eBook promotion websites:

www.bookbub.com
http://ereadernewstoday.com
www.fkbooksandtips.com
www.bookgorilla.com
www.bookblast.co
www.pixelofink.com

Publishing Resources

CreateSpace, for print-on-demand paperbacks:
www.createspace.com
Ingram Spark, an alternative to CreateSpace:
www.ingramspark.com
Kindle Direct Publishing, for Kindle eBooks:
kdp.amazon.com (There is no www.)
Nook Press, for Nook eBooks:
www.nookpress.com
Kobo Writing Life, for Kobo eBooks:
www.kobobooks.com/kobowritinglife
Smashwords, for other eBooks:
www.smashwords.com
Author Central, to create an Amazon author page:
https://authorcentral.amazon.com
https://authorcentral.amazon.co.uk
Community forums and help pages:
www.createspace.com/en/community/index.jspa
https://kdp.amazon.com/community/index.jspa
Copyright and library information:
www.copyright.gov
www.loc.gov
Blogging sites:
www.wordpress.com
www.blogger.com
Social media sites:
www.facebook.com
www.twitter.com
Free and helpful self-publishing resources:
www.chrismcmullen.wordpress.com
Building Your Book for Kindle (Amazon's free guide)
Smashwords Style Guide by Matt Coker
Smashwords Book Marketing Guide by Matt Coker
Secrets to Ebook Publishing Success by Matt Coker

About the Author

CHRIS MCMULLEN HAS written and self-published over a dozen paperback books with Create-Space and over a dozen eBooks. He enjoys writing books, drawing illustrations on the computer, editing manuscripts, and especially the feeling of having produced a professional-looking self-published book from cover-to-cover.

Chris McMullen holds a Ph.D. in physics from Oklahoma State University, and presently teaches physics at Northwestern State University of Louisiana. Having published a half-dozen papers on the collider phenomenology of large, extra, superstring-inspired extra dimensions, he first wrote a two-volume book on the geometry and physics of the fourth dimension geared toward a general audience, entitled *The Visual Guide to Extra Dimensions*. When he learned about self-publishing on Amazon through CreateSpace, he wrote a variety of golf and chess log books, and published these to gain some experience as a self-publisher before self-publishing his work on the fourth dimension.

Since then, Chris McMullen has self-published numerous math workbooks, a few self-publishing books, and several word scramble puzzle books. The math workbooks were written in response to his observation, as a teacher, that many students need to develop greater fluency in fundamental techniques in mathematics. He began writing word scramble books along with his coauthor, Carolyn Kivett, when he realized that it was possible to make over a thousand words using only the elements on the periodic table. Chris McMullen and Carolyn Kivett first published a variety of chemical word scrambles using elements from the periodic table, and have since published several 'ordinary' word scrambles using the English alphabet instead of chemical symbols.

Check out the blog with free self-publishing resources:
www.chrismcmullen.wordpress.com

The author website is:
www.chrismcmullen.com
You can email the author at:
chrism@chrismcmullen.com

The author's Facebook author page is:
www.facebook.com/pages/Chris-Mcmullen
/390266614410127

Follow the author at Twitter:
@ChrisDMcMullen

You can take advantage of a free marketing opportunity
created by Chris McMullen:
www.readtuesday.com

Self-Publishing

How to Self-Publish a Book on Amazon.com
A Detailed Guide to Self-Publishing with Amazon, Vol.'s 1 and 2
Formatting Pages for Publishing on Amazon with CreateSpace

The Fourth Dimension

A Visual Introduction to the Fourth Dimension
The Visual Guide to Extra Dimensions, Vol.'s 1 and 2
Full Color Illustrations of the Fourth Dimension, Vol.'2 1 and 2

Science Books

Understand Basic Chemistry Concepts
An Introduction to Basic Astronomy Concepts (with Space Photos)
An Advanced Introduction to Calculus-Based Physics (Mechanics)
A Guide to Thermal Physics
Creative Physics Problems, Vol.'s 1 and 2

Improve Your Math Fluency Series

Addition Facts Practice Book
Subtraction Facts Practice Book
Multiplication Facts Practice Book
Division Facts Practice Book
10,000 Addition Problems Practice Workbook
10,000 Subtraction Problems Practice Workbook
7,000 Multiplication Problems Practice Workbook
4,500 Multiplication Problems with Answers Practice Workbook
Master Long Division Practice Workbook
Practice Adding, Subtracting, Multiplying, and Dividing Fractions
Practice Arithmetic with Decimals Workbook
Fractions, Decimals, & Percents Math Workbook
Algebra Essentials Practice Workbook with Answers
Trigonometry Essentials Practice Workbook with Answers

Word Scramble Puzzle Books (Coauthored)

Spooky Word Scrambles
Christmas Word Scrambles
Fun Word Scrambles for Kids
Golf Word Scrambles
Teen Word Scrambles for Girls

Self-Publishing Books

A Detailed Guide to Self-Publishing with Amazon and Other Online Booksellers, Volumes 1 and 2

Volume 1 is a detailed, comprehensive guide to self-publishing. It includes numerous tips on formatting the interior and cover for both paperbacks and eBooks, specific instructions for Microsoft Word 2010 (which is very similar to 2007 and 2013) for Windows, and tips for publishing books with CreateSpace, Kindle, Nook, and Smashwords.

Volume 2 provides a thorough introduction to marketing and marketability. It also includes helpful tips for perfecting cover design, paperback formatting, and eBooks as well as a detailed discussion of what authors need to know about Amazon's website.

How to Self-Publish a Book on Amazon.com

This guide to self-publishing covers the basic concepts; it is not nearly as detailed as the author's two-volume set, but covers a wide range of introductory ideas. This book also includes formatting instructions for both Microsoft Word 2003 and 2010 (which is similar to 2007 and 2013).

Formatting Pages for Publishing on Amazon with CreateSpace

This book is specifically geared toward formatting the interior file of a paperback book. Topics include margins, bleed, using both Roman numerals and Arabic numbers, creating multiple headers, formatting text, page layout, borders, widows, orphans, and rivers.

80058011R00104

Made in the USA
San Bernardino, CA
21 June 2018